José Ángel N.

ILLEGAL

Reflections of an Undocumented Immigrant

UNIVERSITY OF ILLINOIS PRESS

Urbana, Chicago, and Springfield

Some of the names and events in this book have been altered.

Library of Congress Cataloging-in-Publication Data
N., José Ángel.
Illegal : reflections of an undocumented immigrant / José Ángel N.
pages cm. — (Latinos in Chicago and Midwest)
ISBN 978-0-252-03831-0 (hardback) — ISBN 978-0-252-07986-3 (paperback) —
ISBN 978-0-252-09618-1 (e-book)
1. N., José Ángel. 2. Illegal aliens—Illinois—Chicago—Biography. 3. Mexicans—
Illinois—Chicago—Biography. 4. United States—Emigration and immigration—
Social aspects. I. Title.
F548.9.M5N3   2014
305.868'720787311—dc23   2013032194

To my wife, D——,
in gratitude

Ambos hechos están relacionados, escribir y destruir,
ocultarse y ser descubierto.

—ROBERTO BOLAÑO

CONTENTS

Foreword by *F. González-Crussi*   ix

1. Amid the Shadows   1
2. Of Things Lost   27
3. My Adult Education   41
4. The Song of the Cicadas   57
5. At Work   77
6. The Day I Got Counted   89

   Postscript   99

FOREWORD

F. González-Crussi

During World War II, just before the American forces disembarked in Sicily, General George S. Patton harangued his men in his inimitable, incisive style, with this caustic oration: "When we land, we will meet German and Italian soldiers whom it is our honor and privilege to attack and destroy. Many of you have in your veins German and Italian blood, but remember that these ancestors of yours so loved freedom that they gave up home and country to cross the ocean in search of liberty. The ancestors of the people we shall kill lacked the courage to make such a sacrifice and continued as slaves."

Thus, the irrepressible general was alluding to an idea that enjoyed much credit in American society at the time, namely, that immigrants represent the most energetic, enterprising, dynamic, and freedom-loving segment of the population of their countries of origin, which they felt compelled to leave. The corollary is that the United States of America would do well to welcome them, as the positive, energizing influence of these opportunity-seeking, active individuals would surely redound to the enhancement of the common weal.

However, a very different view of immigrants was afoot in the land at the same time. This was a hateful, instinctive repulse of the new-comers, more or less arrayed in ideological garb. The expressions of a noted American sociologist of the first part of the twentieth century, Edward Alsworth Ross, were representative of this attitude. His reflections, watching a group of newly arrived southern European immigrants, show that he viewed them as less than admirable. To him, they were "hirsute, low-browed, big-faced persons of obviously low mentality." They were clad in their Sunday best, wishing to make a good impression in their new country, but to Ross they were "out of place" in white shirts of starched collars and black jackets, for he had already adjudicated them as "ox-like men," unfit for fancy clothes and urbane dwellings; rather, they "belonged in skins and wattled huts." Such were the sentiments that the sight of new immigrants elicited in many. These people, mostly Italians, were obviously different from the previous waves of northern white Europeans who had come to America.

The irony of this is, as noted years ago in an article in the *Atlantic Monthly* by David M. Kennedy, a professor of American history at Stanford University, that the people Ross was describing in such unflattering, malicious, and obviously racist terms were the parents of the very troops whom Patton exhorted to battle on the eve of the murderous Sicilian disembarkation in 1943. This point is well worth emphasizing: the human contribution of immigrants is inestimable. However wretched they may appear, human beings are unique, irreplaceable entities. The bestowal of human life has consequences that are, by their very nature, incalculable. Demographic exodus undoubtedly is, on the whole, a grievous loss for the donor country and a gain for the recipient. But it is of a kind that cannot be measured, and therefore it escapes the usual computations of the benefits versus the drawbacks of illegal immigration.

There can be no question about the right of every country to determine who is admitted, when, and how. This is the law, whose present necessity no one could reasonably dispute. Therefore, those who enter or stay in the country illegally (their number in the United States is currently estimated at more than eleven million) are charged with committing a crime. A dictionary definition of *crime* is "the commission of an act that is forbidden or the omission of an act that is commanded by a public law of a sovereign state, to the injury of the public welfare and that makes the offender liable to punishment by that law." In another acceptation, criminal activity is, more generally, "conduct in violation of the law." By these definitions, the number of criminal immigrants living in this country is simply staggering. Yet a natural instinct tells us that this cannot be, that there is a troubling incongruity in applying the same appellation, *criminal,* to a rapist and to a poor, honest gardener, that it is a grotesque nonsense to designate with the same epithet a parricide or a serial killer and a decent, truehearted worker.

Words are powerful tools. They shape attitudes, set expectations, and determine behavior. The language used to characterize undocumented immigrants has cast them almost exclusively in the form of lawbreakers. All human features are effaced by one single trait: their unlawfulness or criminality. This arrant reductionism is being used to justify the most callous abuses against them. We have seen those who lack "papers" to accredit their legality shackled and herded like cattle (significantly, in the much-publicized 2008 raid of a processing plant in Potsville, Iowa, nearly four hundred immigrants were held on the grounds of the National Cattle Congress in Waterloo, Iowa) and then subjected to a judicial process that, in the words of a witness, "resembled a meat-packing assembly line." Here, a few court-appointed defenders offered them complicated plea bargains that most could scarcely understand, but included fast-track deportation. Actions of this ilk, unfortunately far from rare, are fraught with undesirable consequences: homes of innocent people being raided by federal agents acting under mistaken intelligence, citizens being pulled over at roadblocks for no other reason than being dark complexioned, and indiscriminate sweeps at work sites that cause untold misery and unhappiness. Moreover, the police are given powers they are neither meant to have nor trained to fittingly apply. The concerned community becomes intimidated, and therefore less likely to report serious criminal activity to the authorities.

"We have nothing against immigrants; it is the illegal ones we oppose," reads one of the most hackneyed remarks of editorialists. But whoever has seen the plight of those unfortunates at close range will find this comment naive at best and hypocritical at worst. The editorialists' phraseology evokes the image of an orderly line of neatly dressed applicants, attaché cases at their sides, waiting inside the premises of the U.S. Embassy for their turn to solicit a visa to enter the country. The truth is that the uncouth, uneducated, weather-beaten masses of the "unwashed" who aspire to get a menial job in the United States know very well that they don't stand a chance to obtain such a visa. Nor will they come to request one. The consul would ask them to show evidence that they have a bank account, a family estate, or such property as would render it unlikely that they may want to leave their country and reside permanently in the United States. They, in their turn, might retort: "If I had a patrimony, would I be thinking of leaving?" But to be admitted by regular means lacking marketable skills is well nigh impossible. The options are thus limited: to wither indefinitely, barely eking out subsistence wages and pained by the realization that the same closed future awaits one's children, one's wife, and all family dependents, or to risk it all and seek one's chances in a country where the same vexations and hardships endured at home bring a reward five to ten times greater.

The pundits on television and other media generally ignore this fact, that the majority of illegal immigrants come out of their countries like wolves come out of the woods, prompted by hunger. In many cases, *hunger* is a term that applies literally: the urgent, painful awareness of a protracted deprivation of food. In other cases, the word is meant more or less figuratively: the unbearable frustration at seeing that the most legitimate human needs and aspirations—to be educated, to have adequate shelter, to provide for one's family, and so on—must forever be thwarted and remain unfulfilled. Not by bread alone is man's life sustained, and the figurative hunger can be as powerful a determinant as the physiologic. But whether prompted by the one or by the other, the illegal newcomer will be stigmatized as a criminal and doomed to live "amid the shadows."

The shadowy realm is one no one seems ever to look into. Hence the unique appeal of the present book. It is the work of one of those enterprising young men who chose to take a chance and abandon fixed frustration for possible advancement and contingent peril. Whatever the reader may think of this author's outlook, his voice deserves to be heard. He is not looking for sympathy, or appealing for compassion. He came, like millions of others, in search of a better life and never intending to harm anyone. Yet he is fully aware that a large segment of American society concurs in the pronouncement of a prominent anti-immigrant activist who wrote, "The law does not automatically bestow compassion and forgiveness on lawbreakers based on the underlying motives for their crime." Thus, there is no grandstanding in these pages, no affected posturing or ideological advocacy. There is simply the candid narrative of what it means to live *amid the shadows,* and this is done with a rich sensibility and an agile, limpid, engaging writing style. What survival in the shady side implies, we are told, is to live with an ever-present sense of "distance, clandestinity, criminalization, vulnerability, fear, lack of mobility, exclusion, uncertainty, humiliation."

Not the least appeal of this book is that the narrative of a life beset by so many tribulations is told with not a shade of anger or resentment. The dominant tone is one that may be called muted nostalgia, and one that it may not be inappropriate to deem philosophical. The whole is sustained by a lyrical accent, like a melodic refrain, which in some passages we would not hesitate to call poetical. That the author of this excellent book arrived in this country possessed of a very low level of education (incomplete high school) is patent proof of the immense human potential locked in the immigrant population. A country able to use it well would see its efforts amply repaid. In time this population would strengthen the host nation's laws and reinvigorate its arts, and, if not immediately felt, their beneficial influence would bless more distant generations. But what possible advantage can be derived from people constrained to repine under a grinding system that forces them constantly to live in anxiety, amid the shadows?

At the time of this writing, the United States prepares a major overhauling of its immigration laws. It is a core tradition of this country to rectify errors and to stand for what is right, equitable, and just. But, meanwhile, the leaven of intolerance may still be perceived. The anti-immigration groups quibble, declaim, posture, wrangle, denounce, sneer, and calumniate. They form very powerful organizations. Their so-called think tanks wield statistics—that most fickle of tools—undigested facts, and long words. With the cant of jurisprudence, they bewilder the uninformed; with the cant of conventional morality, they baffle the unwary. Meantime, a confused, honest citizenry, upon seeing working mothers shackled, hands tied behind their backs, weeping at not being able to feed their children, exclaims, as did a woman who witnessed a factory raid: "There must be another way! This is not humane."

And the politicians? In their speeches, they quickly pass over the moral problems, out of fear of hindering their own careers. Would that all they skip in their speeches was equally passed over in the world of reality! Political addresses always reflect but a partial view of the problem and systematically elude its painful human aspects. Presidential candidates, inured to public debates, develop a readiness of repartee, a lively eloquence, and an uncanny way of gauging exactly the temper and mood of the audience. With these admirable abilities, they manage to shine by presenting ideas in the media that would never stand attentive, deliberate examination.

All of which points, once again, to the importance of this book. It puts a human face on a whole mass of individuals vowed to invisibility, or at least indistinctness. Their yearnings, perplexities, and hopes are many, yet most of them lack the language, the education, the ability, or the courage to articulate them cogently. But out of these pages rises the voice of one among them, like a voice emerging from the shadows. His words are not the uncompromising utterances of politicians or the sanctimonious banalities that try to appease everyone's good conscience. Rather, it is a voice that says, "I am here, and I am a human being." And by this simple statement, it may shake those who keep deceiving themselves into realizing that it is shameful to abstain from doing what should have been done long ago.

ILLEGAL

ONE
AMID THE SHADOWS

The Jaguar's Path

My life in the shadows began some seventeen years ago. It was a hot April night in Tijuana, that border siren that lures both migrant and tourist with promises of boundless prosperity and unchecked lust. That night I joined a numerous army, an anonymous army. Under the infinite depth of night and guided by a sneaky coyote, we moved, slowly descending the slopes flattened nightly by the illicit weight of millions of other shadows who preceded us. Denied a legitimate chance at the American Dream, what better way to attain it than by penetrating America by night?

There were precedents in my family. Besides a brigade of distant relatives too large to count, two of my maternal uncles had already been to the States. By the time my turn to leave Mexico came, both of them had been back in Guadalajara for almost ten years. Their venture had been a failure, for now they were as broke as they were before leaving. My departure being rushed, we didn't really get a chance to talk about the experience of crossing. So upon leaving, the idea I had of what awaited me was that which I had pieced together overhearing their conversations. If my journey was to resemble theirs, then my trip across the border would be pretty tight and bumpy but safe—I'd be packed, like a sardine, in the trunk of a car among many others. (If things went badly, I'd have to climb over my fellow riders, kick them and push them down as I gasped for the last drops of oxygen, but that was unlikely.) However, reaching my destination safely and quickly was guaranteed. All arrangements had been made ahead of time by a distant relative who had agreed to finance my crossing and hired the reliable services of a reputable coyote.

Thus, after tunneling under that tall, rusty iron curtain that divides both countries, I was surprised. There were no cars waiting. I stood up, dusted off my pants, and looked at the horizon—a dark, endless stretch of hills and valleys appeared before me. I had made the journey with an experienced cousin from Zacatecas whom I had never met before and who didn't bother to inform me of what the crossing would be like. Now, after a ridiculous crawl, I had reached the United States, and I wasn't turning back. I'd follow the coyote's trail.

The stretch between Tijuana and San Diego is long. *Very long.* And it is as treacherous as it is beautiful. It is unlikely that anybody who has ever crossed it will easily forget it. Its desertlike landscape is bound to carve itself equally onto body and soul. Once this turf is trodden, the tiredness, the awe, and the terror experienced along these trails become permanent memories. Some take away a cactus scratch that eventually scars. Others momentarily succumb to the sheer magnitude of the heavens, the number of stars, the depth of night. A few are left behind to join the landscape.

This dark wonder. For many, like myself, this arid world, these steep hills and deep valleys, provides us with our first hike ever. It is also our first view of such broad sky. Our first communion with the infinite. It was probably under pristine and glittering skies like these that Immanuel Kant, bewildered, conceived his mystical dialectic between the starry heavens above and the moral law within. I, lacking all philosophical insight at the time, simply wanted to pause and contemplate this fragment of galaxy. But the coyote had other plans, and we kept pressing forward.

Human industry adds its own accents to the native landscape. From the top of a hill, we watch a long line of people advancing hurriedly in the valley ahead of us. Some two hundred years earlier, pushing westward in this very spot, they would have been considered pioneers. But the journey they have embarked on came too late, and they are not heading west but north, and that alone is their disadvantage and their loss. Or, if they were in other latitudes and times, based on the determination and enthusiasm that fuel their march, one would be inclined to think of them as troops or pilgrims. But here, they are simply shadows.

Suddenly, from a neighboring hill, a series of lights turns on simultaneously. Some come from trucks parked at ground level. Others descend, flickering rapidly like a furious shower of shooting stars. For those unfortunate souls, this is as far as the American Dream will go.

Way up on top, we duck and hide. We wait.

How long we spend perched on top of that hill afterward I can't tell. Before the incident below, I reckon we have been going for more than an hour. All I know is I'm glad we stopped. A smoker at the time, I feel dizzy, my lungs are swelling, my nostrils flare rapidly, my legs are getting heavier, and I am drenched in sweat. The coyote squats and hisses at us not to move, gesticulating violently and pointing to the ground with his right hand.

I land on my stomach and crawl my way into a narrow space between a big rock and a thorny bush. The backpack in which I carry a change of clothes, a bottle of water, and some snacks is wet with sweat, and I feel a pointy rock stabbing me right in the stomach, but remain motionless. I am panting heavily and fear that my breathing will attract a rattlesnake. A few minutes pass, and someone close by begins to snore. I keep my eyes open.

The noise and commotion below eventually subside, but the coyote whispers, warning us not to move yet. I hear the car engines pull away and feel relieved. We keep waiting. More noises in the distance. A helicopter! A different group is being hunted down on another hill. With a little bit of luck, those two groups will keep the *migras* busy as we resume our journey.

We move on and keep going for what seems to be a very long time. We run and I keep coughing. We go up and down hills that never seem to end. At some point, running upward along a narrow path, I look down the cliff to my right and feel nauseated. It is a long, rocky fall. All it would take for my journey to be over would be a momentary distraction, a trip on a rock, a slip, someone accidentally bumping me from behind. How many dreams have ended like this, way down there?

We descend again, and I am glad to hear the coyote say, "¡Ya estuvo, ya la hicimos!" I hear him and feel relieved and share in the collective enthusiasm. People say "¡Órale!" and "¡Chido!" and "¡Ya chingamos!" but I still don't understand how it is that we have actually "made it." This valley looks as deserted as any other we have passed.

Reaching the bottom of the next hill, the coyote takes out a flashlight and points it with his commanding right hand. And then I see it, the miracle of this Mexican Moses who promises to deliver us from the Jaguar's oppression materializes in front of me—a dark circle opens up ahead, like a surreal toothless mouth, threatening to devour us.

Had the other two groups made it this far, the *migras* would have never caught up with them. No *migra* would ever go down this pipe. Nobody with any human dignity would, so we leave ours behind.

We enter the dark cylindrical hole, and I say to myself, so this it, this is what it means to have made it. The pipe is about five feet in height. We duck and enter the filthy bowels of San Diego where rodents make their home and humans are unwelcome invaders. The air inside is heavy and damp, and there is a pungent stench to it. I stretch my arms to the sides to find support on the inner walls of the pipe. My hands feel wet and sticky. I feel helpless. Amid the constant sound of shoes hitting the metal below, I sob quietly. Traveling in the same direction, narcotics on their way to give a high to those who vilify my journey are transported in a much more humane and sanitary fashion. The humiliation I experience is so deep I promise myself that if I am ever caught, I will never try crossing again.

Eventually, the darkness ends. We come out, and one by one we all collapse on the ground. I feel exhausted and sick. My back hurts, and I wonder if I'll ever be able to stand straight up again.

: : :

CHAPTER ONE

My first real sighting of the United States is that of a major highway down below. If I were to measure it across, it would easily be about two blocks of my hometown. I stare at it in awe, almost frightened by its sheer width. The coyote has given us a few minutes to recover, and now we are ready to move on. We cross that highway on a bridge above. A peaceful park welcomes us. Crossing the park, we reach the parking lot of a school, and, just past it, we encounter the first houses.

An unsuspecting sense of tranquillity guards the sleep of this pleasant American suburb. It is dark, and the silent peace is broken only by the echo of our steps.

Like thieves, we prowl through the night.

Crossing the border is a complicated business. At first I am so physically exhausted and afraid of being caught that I can't think of anything other than reaching my destination. But soon new feelings take shape. Entering a place uninvited implies a breach of trust. It stirs conflicting emotions and opens up room for moral ambivalence.

So far in my journey, I have felt only humiliated and robbed of human dignity. But now, breaking into someone else's backyard at night, I've become an intruder, and it shames me deeply. Though I don't know it at the time, I now suppose this is why the good, law-abiding American citizen clings so fiercely to his guns. If he discovered us, he'd have the full recourse of the law behind him to take a few of us down, invaders that we are. And wouldn't I do the same when it came to protecting the peaceful sleep of my own children?

The coyote directs us to a garden hose for a drink of water. But, good Mexican that I am, I know not to *ever* drink running water. I unzip my backpack and take out the bottle I carry with me. I drink the remaining water in one single gulp. And, after a moment of doubt and moral speculation, after being seized by feelings of guilt and shame, I chuckle. I take the plastic bottle, crush it with my right hand, and toss it onto the perfectly clean green lawn. A souvenir. A harmless weapon abandoned by an advancing horde of shadows.

When we get to a small strip mall, there are a couple of vans waiting for us. We get in and are driven away. The house where we are taken is small and filthy, and it is so full with people you'd think nobody else could fit inside it. But they make room for us. Other than a kitchen table and a few chairs, there is no furniture whatsoever. I stink and want to shower but am told I can't. The food they serve us is bland and cold, but we eat it all the same. We are not allowed to go out to the backyard, let alone leave the house. There is a television in the living room, and we all sit around to watch it. The guy sitting next to me leaves, and I am so tired I recline on the filthy carpet and pass out immediately.

As the day progresses, people come and go, taking some of those who made the journey with us. Nobody comes for me and my cousin or for a few others until the next day, when we are taken to a different house. We wait around for a few hours, and I feel bored and restless. I want to get out, move about, walk through the neighborhood. Then it happens—from the room where we sit around looking at each other, we hear a loud noise, and the front door is kicked open. We freeze, and a tall Hispanic man dressed in green comes in first, ordering, "Nadie se mueve!"

: : :

Being in jail is not as scary as they make you think. At least not the jail I am taken to. I expect beatings, interrogations. But instead, when my time comes to make a statement, I am kindly led to a desk where a blond officer sits. In a Spanish that impresses me, he asks me my full name and place and date of birth, whether I have tried crossing before and if I'll try again afterward. I say no to both, and I don't remember if he either makes me sign a document or takes my fingerprints. (Many years later, my bad memory will haunt me. A lawyer I consult will insist that this detail is crucial. Not knowing whether I signed a voluntary deportation note could potentially make a difference when trying to get my papers.)

Back in my cell, I look at the others—our eyes bear a single sadness, a single disappointment. I have been told by those who can fly that the trip from Guadalajara to Chicago is about four hours long. Counting from the moment I departed from Guadalajara, about four full days have passed, and I feel frustrated and exhausted. We sit in silence until an officer comes and opens the cell. He pushes in a cart filled with sandwiches, chips, and soda. His civility and kindness confuse me and make me suspicious. The treatment we receive at the detention center is much better than that offered by the ring of smugglers, one of whose operators now sits right next to me. Looking at us with sympathy, the officer suddenly says, in a playful and encouraging voice, "¡Órale cabrones, muevan la nalga, por eso los agarran!"

Hours later, having fed us and taken everyone's statements, they herd us onto a bus where others are already waiting. We are driven out of the detention center, and soon I see myself traveling along one of those amazing highways that were my first sight of real America. Not long after, we see a cluster of high-rises. Someone says it is downtown Los Angeles. I remember this is a sight I have always wanted to see, but under different circumstances.

Reaching the border, we are released and go back to the hotel where we spent a few hours when we first arrived in Tijuana. That very night, I break the promise I had made to myself—I disappear into the deep night of San Diego again.

In the Land of the Free

In subsequent chapters, I will describe in greater detail the events that have taken place since I crossed the border successfully the second time around, events that may make it seem as though my story embodies the fairy tale of the American Dream: learning English, working numerous jobs, getting my GED, putting myself through college and grad school, and becoming a professional translator who now owns a condo in a luxury high-rise overlooking the city. For a young adult who left his native Guadalajara with nothing more than a ninth grade education and a large debt to pay for his smuggling, achieving each of these goals has been highly rewarding, each one more meaningful than the one before.

But this is all the nice part of my story, and what I am interested in telling in the following pages is something quite different—the story behind the mirage of my accomplishments.

If I could tell it with a riddle, it would go something like this: What climbs toward the light only to be engulfed in gloom? Answer: the undocumented.

:::

I've grown used to living in the shadows. Although it is plagued with inconveniences, I've learned to embrace this lifestyle whole-heartedly. If I had to, I'd choose to live it all over again—every single moment of it! I've come to appreciate the anonymity. I love the permissiveness to slip in and out of places virtually unnoticed. Plus, this subterranean life offers other advantages. Like evolution.

There is ample room for growth in the shadows. Although it took me a long time, I have finally realized that one can actually thrive in the shadows as well as anywhere else. Except that down here you evolve differently—you become darker, you grow antennae, your senses get sharper, and, best of all, you learn not to take things so seriously.

But this sardonic wisdom comes only with time. It is only after you have been engaging in the business of descending to explore the shadows and going back up to greet the light again that the whole transition from one world to the other becomes joyful. A pleasant seesaw ride.

Although my expedition into this world of shadows started long ago, only within the past few years have I reached its final depths. In a strange twist of irony, this last descent of mine started simultaneously with my climb toward the American middle class. Pulled in both directions, I have become a hybrid creature of darkness and hope, one who can scratch the heights of prosperity but who remains permanently rooted in misfortune.

In a way, my life since has been a strange negation of Plato's allegory—the chains that used to bind me are now broken, but I never left my imprisonment. I stayed back in the cave, amid the shadows. Add that to my private nature, and what you get is a painting by Caspar David Friedrich, except that the landscape is bustling downtown Chicago, where I wander about.

I started lurking in the lowest ring of these depths after landing my current job, some five years ago. My years of adult education and my intensive study of both my native and my new languages finally paid off, and I went from serving tables to the comfort of an air-conditioned office. I found a job as a professional translator. Dress shoes and a tie. Back then I never imagined that things around me would get gradually darker. Everything seemed promising. The way things looked, it'd be a matter of a year or two before my legal dilemma got solved. I was going through a hopeful period in my life, and things were changing rapidly. Within a month of starting my new job, downtown Chicago was taken aback, as the chants of a half-million shadows echoed through its financial district. Back in Washington, they took notice. Congress debated an immigration reform bill that was sure to pass.

At about the same time, less than a year into my new job, I was offered a promotion. It would require that I travel several times a year. Los Angeles, New York, Miami. They were even thinking of sending me down to Mexico!

That was the summit of my life in the States, and it was exactly then that my final descent started. I'd been seduced by the charms of Fortune, and now I had to bear her disdain.

Citing the precarious health of a family member, I declined the promotion. There was no ill family member. I would have been willing to accept the position, if I could only travel. The bill that Congress debated at the time had just met its demise at the happily clapping hands of Republicans, making it impossible for me to comply with the traveling requirements my new position would require.

The morning I declined the promotion, I woke up unusually early. I don't know what time it was, but it was still dark out. I woke up but did not get up. Lying in bed, I looked outside and saw a plane go by. With no exception, all planes I see from my window are arrivals, many of which come from overseas. They head westward toward O'Hare Airport after treating passengers to a view of Chicago's amazing lakeshore and skyline.

With all its splendor, with its wings widespread and its shining armor, that plane seemed to be plotting against my pride. I felt secretly insulted by it. Its flashing lights, I was sure, were mocking me. Shortly after, the plane disappeared from the horizon. I had just read an article saying that about half of all undocumented immigrants enter the country legally, and I wondered how many passengers on that plane would eventually join me in the shadows. Overstaying one's visa is as common as crossing the scorching Arizona desert. How many of those visas would be left to expire? How many, seduced by abundant luxuries and comfort, would find the legal loophole of marriage and ditch this world of shadows altogether?

After about an hour, I had counted a total of seven planes. I decided to get up, and a punctual literary thought came to me. It was a reflection by a highly imaginative and passive Frenchman. Blaise Pascal wrote that all the problems of a man come as a result of his inability to sit quietly at home. I felt a bittersweet sensation of guilt and satisfaction. If it was true that in leaving Mexico I had summoned all the want, humiliation, and gloom that surrounded me, then it was also true that staying put in Chicago would spare me the remaining evils of the universe.

Going forward, Pascal's maxim would be my guiding principle.

: : :

During my first years in Chicago, I didn't know Pascal. Nor did I need to. The educational opportunities before me were appealing enough to convince me to stick around in Chicago. I knew that I might not be able to come back to the States if I ever left, so I learned to count that limitation among my blessings. Accepting my inability to travel saved me from the fate of many of my countrymen. I was spared the vicious yearly cycle of crossing the border, working two jobs, saving enough money, going back to Mexico, getting smuggled back into the States, and depositing the fruit of my labor in the greedy claws of the coyote.

While some of the cooks at the Mexican restaurant where I worked at the time came and went, I stayed put in Chicago. I had been studying English for a while now and had found the activity thoroughly engaging. I focused on the conjugation of verbs, the placement of adjectives, the construction of sentences, paragraph structure. Upon their return the following year, the cooks found me coming back from classes with my GED book under my arm.

I was fully immersed in the study of basic math, natural science, and American history. As my reading of American history progressed, I found consolation to my legal limbo in the experience of previous waves of immigrants. According to my readings, they had become exemplary citizens through assimilation, the melting pot, and prosperity, all of which, my books told me, were within my reach. Those were the happy times when, according to his fabled account of America's idyllic past, Professor Samuel Huntington tells us that "immigrants wept with joy when, after overcoming hardship and risk, they saw the Statue of Liberty; enthusiastically identified themselves with their new country that offered them liberty, work, and hope." Of course, reading passages like this now after many years, I remember my own coming to America and realize that there was nothing sentimental about it, nothing to move me to tears. There was only an urgent and concrete need, a physical need that I first relieved myself of with a warm, arching fluid that cascaded against the rusty fence I crawled under. And because of the mischief of having entered through the back door and because I arrived too late and from a country so close by that my language and culture are easy to retain, Professor Huntington is convinced that I am utterly ungrateful, disloyal, and unappreciative. Seized by a nativist paranoia, he deems me a threat to American identity.

But when I first found out I could obtain my GED, I didn't know any of this, and all I wanted was an education. However, as time passed, and thanks to the lessons contained in my fat GED book, I began to see myself in the social fabric of the United States. I was becoming aware of my role in its landscape. A dishwasher at the time, though, what contributions could I make to society other than mastering the skill of swift and meticulous plate washing? What threat could I pose other than dropping a basket full of dishes or sending bean-stained silverware to greet customers in the dining room?

If I wanted to become part of this society, continuing with my studies seemed the most sensible idea. So, years later when I started college, I dedicated endless hours to studying for my college courses and grad seminars while working full-time all the while. Yet once I completed grad school about ten years later, Congress, that shrine of benevolence I read about in awe in my books, decided to surprise me.

The law Congress passed was known as the Real ID Act, and it required anyone renewing his driver's license to provide a valid Social Security number. Like that of most undocumented immigrants I know, my Social Security number was a made-up number. One Sunday afternoon, shortly after arriving in Chicago, I had taken a trip to 26th Street. There, like characters out of a movie, Mexican guys lean against the walls of buildings—their hands in their front pockets, a foot resting flatly on the wall—and whisper furtively to pedestrians, "Seguros, micas, micas . . ."

Unlike my Social Security number, the driver's license I went on to get a few weeks later was a valid one. How exactly that worked in the United States, a country with lofty ideals of moral purity, I have no idea. But one should remember that corruption has a way of seeping into every crevice and that not even the United States, in spite of its zeal to rid the world of corrupt regimes, is impervious to it. All I know is that by the time I had my driver's license in my hands, the original debt I had to pay for my clandestine passage into the United States had more than doubled.

Although the Real ID Act was aimed at cracking down on terrorists, its claws scratched me too. By then, many years after having arrived in the United States, I had climbed the ladder of success at the restaurant. I was then a waiter, and that was unacceptable for Congressman James Sensenbrenner of Wisconsin, the proponent of the law. It was reason enough to see me with suspicion. He deemed me among those sowing havoc and terror. I had infiltrated the dining room. I had new and greater powers. I now ran amok between tables on busy Friday nights. I threatened to put in the wrong order, to deny someone another basket of chips and salsa, to spill a strawberry margarita on a customer's shirt!

Mr. Sensenbrenner took notice of this. And, like Moses, he stretched out his mighty hands and brought Darkness to bear upon Chicago—the Chicago where I live.

Since the passage of the Real ID Act about five years ago, the circle of my mobility has been gradually shrinking. My environment has changed significantly. It's gotten darker. Tighter. This action by

Congress pushed me deeper into the shadows. So much so that I've been gradually disappearing.

Within a year of the law's passage, the investment I had made stopped yielding interest. I was no longer able to renew my driver's license, so I sold my car and disappeared from the roads. I used to go in and out of bars without any worries, and now I disappeared from those cheerful places as well.

At first, the prospect of being without a single legal document worried me. I started to feel trapped. I got depressed. My driver's license would expire a little more than a year after grad school. I'd been looking forward to this time. I expected to enter a new and promising phase of my life. And I did, since I found my current job a year or so after grad school. But within a few months of getting my current job, I no longer had any valid legal documents.

:::

A few months later, in the parking lot of a Jewel at an undisclosed location, Mario noticed how particular and demanding I was. Keeping all the same details was extremely important. He looked at me attentively. He nodded and said he could do almost everything I asked, but he wasn't sure he could keep a serial number running along the edge. He thought the template in his computer program might be permanent. And one thing he was sure he could not reproduce was the hologram, "El único pedo es que todavía no podemos hacerlas brillar así."

A few days later, Mario pulled up at a Walgreen's parking lot downtown. Riding in the back with him was a boy about five or six years old and an older lady. I approached the car and saw them snacking. What a beautiful family! Such genius! Who would ever suspect anything? Mario retrieved an envelope and handed it to me. I verified the information. Everything was as requested. I gave him the balance and watched them take off.

It was not perfect, but at least this new driver's license of mine would not expire until several years into the future. Plus, it had a new picture.

Sensenbrenner might have obscured the skies, but he forgot to seal the sewers.

By the time I got this new driver's license, I had just moved into my condo on the north side of the city where public transportation is pretty decent, so I had no more need to drive. My only goal in obtaining this license was not to feel so isolated and singled out. Pretty much like the way minors do, I'd use it exclusively whenever I wanted to get into a bar, or, like a drunk, buy some booze and go home to drink alone. So, a few days after I got it, I went to the liquor store I'd been going to for the past few years. After getting my usual two bottles of wine, I stood in line at the cash register. When I handed the cashier my driver's license, she stared at it, twisting it and angling it toward the light. I knew she was a new employee because I had never seen her there before. So I told her that I'd always used that ID there. She had already scanned my loyalty card, and the accrued points on my account should be evidence that I was a longtime customer. I was sure this would dissipate any doubts she might still have. But she didn't listen. Instead, she turned to her supervisor and asked him to have a look at it.

Busy amid a hectic crowd, he took a quick glance and gestured disapprovingly. He too found it awkward. He shook his head and echoed her, saying it looked weird. He then turned to me. I don't know if he recognized me, but my week-old beard surely convinced him of my age. He drew a complicit smirk—yes, he'd let me buy my wine, but I wasn't fooling him. He knew full well I carried a fake document. But I was lucky—no liberal gringo in this part of town would embarrass a man from an ethnic minority any further. He wouldn't call the police on me. He'd simply let this one minute in the spotlight of shame be my lesson. I stood there, a line of five or six inquisitive and impatient people waiting behind me. The adjacent cashiers were just as busy, and the people standing in line on both sides gave me strange looks. Now my accomplice, the manager, authorized the purchase. I handed my credit card to the cashier and signed my receipt. Then, humiliated and with a knot in my throat, I stepped out of the liquor store and into an unusually cold autumn night.

That night I decided I would not be humiliated or ridiculed again. Next time, when carded, I'd simply produce my *matrícula,* an official document issued by the Mexican government that basically identifies you as undocumented. The first time I tried it, no one gave me any problems, so I decided I'd use it everywhere. The only disadvantage is that using my *matrícula* has placed me out of the circle of my coworkers. Now, every time they ask me to join them for a drink, I have to politely decline, citing some previous engagement, tiredness, and so on.

The majority of my coworkers would instantly recognize my illegality if they saw my *matrícula.* They all have a cousin, a brother-in-law, a friend, or a neighbor in a similar situation and accept their illegality as a nuisance. But for their coworker to be undocumented would be a completely different matter. What would they think of me, their colleague?

If we only shared a different occupation, if we sweated right next to each other at an assembly line or at a kitchen grill, perhaps their opinion of me would be different. There would be more room for brotherhood. A broader understanding. A common cause. One single struggle rooted in our working-class condition.

But to find out that an undocumented has infiltrated their office, that I sit at the desk right next to them? What if my salary is higher? The fact that I might have better qualifications would not matter. Their indignation would trump their sympathy. In their eyes, I would cease to be their coworker. They'd probably see in me only the criminal. The trespasser.

Thus far, I have successfully declined their rare invitations for a drink. No one suspects anything.

For a time, while away from my coworkers, using my *matrícula* and not having to worry about being caught with a fake driver's license gave me great peace of mind. It restored my confidence. As long as I proceeded this way, I'd be fine. I had adapted successfully. I had gotten used to the darkness, to this covert world. I had become quite good at secrecy and quietness. I had become acquainted with the art of patience. All I needed was to continue like this, to master Pascal's principle. Be disciplined. Circumscribe myself to this safety circle.

In addition, I had already been residing in the shadows for more than thirteen years. I'd recently suffered a couple of setbacks with the passage of the Real ID Act and the frustrated legalization attempt. But I considered these to be minor obstacles along the way. They would not disturb me. I'd soldier on to the major battle, the one that would solve my situation once and for good.

However, the safety I felt using my *matrícula* was to be short-lived. Once, walking down the liquor aisle at a grocery store, I saw a really good Cabernet on special. Chocolate, spices, cherries . . . The description was so appealing and the price so right for my budget, I didn't think twice before getting it.

At the register, the cashier asked me for an ID. I handed her my *matrícula*. She stared at it momentarily. She then raised her dark eyes and said, with an irritated and authoritative voice, with all the contempt the inner-city working class feel for the immigrant, especially the undocumented, "An *Ameeeerican* ID, sir!"

That Saturday evening, a glass of milk accompanied my dinner.

Another time, more than two years later, while enjoying a new and exciting American experience at a baseball park, I approached the beer man. With a big smile and a kind voice, he asked for my ID. I looked in my wallet, found my *matrícula,* and handed it to him. He took it and held it between his right index finger and thumb.

He looked at it. He studied my picture carefully. Saw my bald head, my intense look. He read the capital letters of my national origin, and the expression on his face began to change. And with good reason. Seconds earlier he had been pouring a nectar of the purest joy, and now he found himself serving *me* a bitter drink. His voice became deeper; his tone was no longer jovial but sententious. His eyebrows drew closer to one another. Towering over me from his six-foot-plus height, he looked down and said, "Put that thing away. I never saw it."

He then handed it back to me, my little green Star of David.

Standing right next to me, my girlfriend looked at me with her compassionate eyes. She didn't say anything, nor did she need to. We both knew that scenes like this were bound to happen, and somehow her silence was reassuring. I looked into her loving deep blue eyes and found the strength and the solace I would invariably gravitate toward in years to come, whenever the burden of my situation became unbearable.

Still, the stigma I felt at the moment didn't go away. I took my *matrícula* from the vendor's hand, feeling ashamed and worthless. I looked at this good man in the eye for a second, and I couldn't help feeling guilty. I had implicated him in a moral offense, in a conspiracy, in the grave crime of my illegality. What would happen to this honest, working-class man if his superiors found out? What would it take, a fellow beer seller walking by?

I was also afraid. What if he decided to walk up to the Chicago police officers standing not far from us and denounce me directly? Had I ruined his evening?

Later, during the game, I saw him again. He was a few steps down the stairs, performing his job with genuine happiness. "Here you go, buddy," he said in a loud and cheerful voice, handing back an ID to his young customer. He looked up my way but didn't see me. My presence had made him uncomfortable only minutes before, when we first crossed paths. But I was no longer visible, and thus I was easily forgotten. I had disappeared from the horizon of his concerns. I had been nothing more than a momentary annoyance, and now I wasn't even that. Like every undocumented man, woman, and child, I was nothing more than a ghost. I had no concrete existence—I had disappeared amid the cheerful multitudes of America, amid this cheering crowd whose home team had just scored.

Sitting to my right, my future wife rooted and clapped. I looked at her and smiled. There was so much we would have to go through in the years to come. But for the moment, I was no longer a threat; I was no longer a burden. So I sat back, drank my beer slowly, and enjoyed this most American of experiences.

Paid Vacation

In a phone message, my friend Francisco asked me to take over an interpretation job for him the following morning. He was flying off to Paris with his girlfriend in a few minutes and wouldn't be able to see it through. A last-minute trip, he said. Unexpected. I called him and left him a message, asking him to provide the details of the job, what the nature of it was, and where it'd take place.

Hours later he texted me: federal building, great pay, thirty-five minutes only, confirm.

I reached him at the Avenue des Champs-Elysées taking a walk with his girlfriend. Because he knows about my situation, I told him that my driver's license had recently expired and that going into a federal building with a fake ID would probably get me deported. He answered with a dead-cold silence. I felt that I had ruined a perfect moment for him, a perfect walk holding hands with his girlfriend.

Poor Francisco. He's never experienced the pangs of illegality. Did I make him feel sorry for me? Was it too abrupt, telling him about my latest problem? I imagined a bitter taste suddenly rushing up his throat, and I felt guilty. Maybe he had plans of proposing to his girlfriend right there, in that most romantic of cities, and I'd probably just ruined his mood. Did he imagine himself in my position, this happy, garrulous, and free spirit?

Born in the same city as me, Francisco has always experienced the world as an open place. Thanks to a combination of factors and to his girlfriend who gets him free plane tickets, during the past couple of years he has been to Maui, Osaka, London, Santiago de Chile, Mexico City, La Paz, Berlin, Amsterdam, and Madrid, among other places. I have seen the pictures, so I know it's true.

Imagine this generous, noble soul who called to offer me an easy job suddenly filled with empathy and engulfed in a sea of sadness!

Or not.

Maybe he simply held his girlfriend's hand tighter and looked up and forward upon the Avenue des Champs-Elysées, its long stretches, its ancient architecture, its long rows of trees, not giving any more thought to a conversation that was utterly irrelevant to him.

: : :

Thomas Carlyle once wrote that a man can never meet his fate if he is not allowed to do his job. A year into my new job and with no one interfering between it and me, I had come to think of my position as a translator as my real calling—I *was* meeting my fate. Or so I thought.

Although my job was to connect two worlds, a strange twist of irony decided that the gap between my professional and my inner life would become more and more unbridgeable as time went by. One of the pitfalls of my humble success, of my clandestine revolt from the shadows, is that, by becoming a professional, I have also become a much sadder man.

In an earlier section, I mentioned how I fear that my coworkers at the office will find out about my situation. Along with that fear also comes a sense of oppression. My years as a working professional have made me feel imprisoned. During my first years in Chicago, working at a restaurant, sweating side by side with my undocumented brethren, I had nothing to fear. Nothing oppressed me. Nothing embarrassed me. We all shared a common story, a common background, a common vocabulary that in many ways I found lacking as I entered my new life. The vocabulary of leisure travel, for instance, was never part of our conversations. Leisure travel was the province of luckier folks. It was an experience none of us had ever had and therefore one that we never talked about. We knew about smuggling, crossing the border at night, swimming across the river, being transported in a trunk, being raided, incarcerated, and deported. But *passports, airports, landings, connections,* and *missed flights* were terms conspicuously absent from our lexicon.

Only during those years did I feel I was earning my bread with pride and honesty. But now things are different.

Although I've paid dearly for acquiring the skills required for this job and I'm quite comfortable performing it, I can never feel completely at ease. I can't help feeling like an intruder. The compensation at my current job is much better, but that can't buy tranquillity. It can't alleviate the constant nervousness. It can't remove the threat of Damocles' sword hanging above my head. As though I were made for them, only when performing menial chores have I felt completely at ease. True, back then I was poorer. But at least I was at more liberty to be myself. I was less isolated, less stigmatized, less anxious.

When I first got my current job, besides the advantage of much better pay and a desk, another great benefit I was entitled to was a weeklong paid vacation during my first year of employment. By the time I took my first paid vacation ever, I was almost thirty-five years old. As I looked forward to it, a genuine excitement and a sense of accomplishment stirred within me. What else could I ask of America? I, who one night had sneaked through her back door, was now being extended this one benefit exclusive to her first-class citizens.

At times, America's generous hand is so long and bright, it can reach the darkest depths.

Of course, I had no illusions, no plans of going anywhere. During my first two years at work, whenever someone asked me where I'd be vacationing, I'd simply say nowhere. I would tell them I was planning a big trip to Europe, but I needed to accrue more vacation time, save enough money, plan well. And this would take a couple of years. Thus, the first two years went by without any problems. By the third year, however, people started getting curious. The questions became more frequent. They wanted to know where I'd be landing, Paris or London? Was I planning a shorter trip during the summer?

At around this time, Michael, a coworker, invited people from the office to his house. It was a nice dinner. He and his wife travel constantly. I admired and envied their picture collection. It extends far and wide: from Jerusalem to Santo Domingo. Showing me his latest pictures in Rio, he asked how my plans for Europe were going. How long had it been since I'd been to Mexico? Why didn't I join them with a group of other people for their next weekend trip to Yellowstone? It was still a month and a half away, more than enough time to make plans and find tickets on the same flight.

Sure, I'll let you know, I answered, smiling broadly.

The following year, having accumulated enough vacation time and having run out of excuses for not going on vacation, I invented one for myself. I told those who asked that I was going to visit my family in Mexico in early January and stay there for about two weeks.

I didn't go anywhere. For a whole week, I stayed home, warmly dressed and happy not have to go out in the arctic cold that subdued Chicago those days. When Sunday came, though, the city experienced an unusually high temperature for that time of the year. I decided to go out, but I needed to hide from my coworkers, many of whom live in my neighborhood and whom I invariably run into strolling down Michigan Avenue on the weekends.

I needed a plan. So, as though it were still cold, I bundled up before leaving the house. I put on a hoodie, a winter hat, an old but warm coat I never wore. I wrapped the thickest of my scarves around my neck—it hid half my face and my nose, leaving only my eyes uncovered. Nobody would recognize me like this. I could stand right next to any of my coworkers, and they would have no idea that it was I. To prove it, I actually *hoped* to run into one of them. With all my layers, I'd walk in front of them and then back, taking small, heavy, bouncing steps, like one wearing an astronaut's suit.

Ah, my vacation! It served only to accentuate my solitude, to remind me of my illegality, to oppress me even more.

Strolling along Michigan Avenue, a group of tall, young athletes went by wearing only shorts and light fleeces. One of them looked my way. And, like some playful and childish giant, he pointed down at me with his right index finger and laughed aloud. With a high adolescent pitch, he muttered something, mocking me. I felt embarrassed and began sweating even more underneath my winter clothes.

The day before I was supposed to go back to work I prepared my answers. I had had a great trip. Spending time with my family was wonderful: my brothers and I went to a punk concert, a soccer game, and the Instituto Cultural Cabañas to see José Clemente Orozco's murals. I visited relatives, saw old friends, listened to an awesome mariachi in Tlaquepaque with my mother, bought her crafts in Tonalá, went to see la Virgen de Zapopan, and so on.

I told my coworkers I came back from Guadalajara just in time to watch Barack Obama being sworn into office. I told them I wanted to watch the whole ceremony, the crowds gathering in D.C. . . . What I really looked forward to, which I didn't tell them, was listening to President Obama's speech, hearing him say, again, that the realm of shadows I inhabited would soon dispel—that would be the perfect way to end my vacation!

: : :

The cornucopia of life is so full of surprises. Its generosity handed me my current job, and its indifference robbed me of my freedom of movement. It also gives abundantly to some what it denies to others. I returned to work, telling my coworkers I had cut my vacation short to come see Obama's inauguration. By a strange twist of fate, a few months later President Obama went to Guadalajara (¡*Guadalajara!*) on his first official trip to Mexico.

How proud I felt of my city! I showed my coworkers the picture of the presidents in the colonial patio of the Instituto Cultural Cabañas, just where *I* was not too long ago. There they sat, the three leaders of North America—Calderón, Obama, and Harper—the Three Amigos, some witty reporter wrote.

What a sight: the clear blue skies, the beautiful patio, the table adorned with colorful Mexican motifs, the blown-glass pitcher, the woven *tortillero*, the handmade *equipales*, the mariachi that doesn't appear in the picture because serious business was being discussed at the moment.

Only after the security, prosperity, and growth of our region were agreed upon did the mariachi play "Cielito lindo."

Did you listen to it, Mr. Obama? Did you hear that amorphous voice? Was it some demon shrieking through José Alfredo's throat, or was it Javier Solís, the velvet voice of Mexico who was taken away from us so prematurely? Whose echo did you hear bouncing off our sorrow? And Orozco's rendering, did you see that man rising up in flames?

So much to hear, so much to see and ponder!

No, unlike Mr. Obama, I did not walk under the clear blue skies of my native Guadalajara. I did, however, get to see my family.

After numerous failed attempts over several weekends, my brother and I finally established a decent connection through Skype. His face looked young and radiant. His forehead was broad, and the light coming in from the back patio seemed to gather there. The image on the screen froze momentarily, but it was restored almost immediately. And, as though resuming a conversation we'd left off at some point in the recent past, I asked him how everything was going at school. How was everything going with our youngest brother's band? When did he play last? Where?

We talked about some of their favorite bands. He made some comment about our local *fútbol* team. He mentioned some conference he'd have to attend for school. He then spun his chair and said something to someone who wasn't there. Briefly after, my mother opened the door and walked into his bedroom and said to me, "¡Hijo, por fin te veo!"

Seventeen years had passed since we'd last seen each other face-to-face. In more than one sense, though, my mother was still the same woman who had seen me off at the bus terminal in Guadalajara. Her sad, brown eyes, accustomed to early departures, her mouth, always hesitant to smile too much and too jovially. My brother opened the blinds, and I saw her more clearly: some gray hairs tangled around her curls, and the first signs of aging adorned her brow. She bit her lower lip. I asked her what she'd just been doing, and she answered laundry, as usual. She lifted up the lower end of her apron and wiped her right cheek. Always self-conscious of her appearance, she added, "Ay, qué fachas las mías." She shook her head slightly, fixed her hair, and took off her apron, apologizing for not having done so before.

Mocking me, she made some remarks about my shaved head. Then she was worried about the weight I had lost recently. Was I eating well? Was I sick? I smiled for her, and she noticed the gaps in my teeth, wider now than in a picture she kept of me as a teenager.

I'm a different man now, Mamá, and not only in appearance. My whole life has been transformed during all these years away from home.

I stand by the tall window of my seventh-floor condo in this luxury high-rise and look outside—Chicago's skyline is so broad, and it promises so much . . . Things I would have never dreamed about when I first arrived in this city. When I come home from work, a man in a suit behind a desk touches his hat with his fingertips and greets me. He pushes a button and opens the door for me. He calls me "Sir."

My personality has also changed. By going to college, I acquired a taste for a dimension of culture I never knew about before. Now I have a special penchant for all things German, from the music of Telemann to the writings of Theodor W. Adorno.

Also now, rather than going to rowdy weekend gatherings with relatives, I have come to appreciate the lonely and quiet times at home. Here, I pour myself a glass of Carménère. I put some music on and let the wine work its wonders. Tonight, Leonard Cohen has kept me company; a single song of his has been playing in an endless loop for more than an hour. I like to sit here and go over the highlighted passages of some texts I read in college: The Laws of Manu, the Upanishads, the Vedas, the Gita—the whole wisdom of ancient India flowing right here on my coffee table.

Whenever my illegality gets particularly difficult, I pull these books down from the top shelf. These books provide me with comfort— they are excellent manuals on the virtues of humility and resignation. Some of their pages tell me that the contradictions and burdens and achievements and frustrations and everything else in life are only an illusion. And they must be, for after leafing through those pages for a while, I can muster the courage to ask questions like, *What is so terrible about being undocumented?*

Indian philosophy might very well be true. I reach for a piece of cheese and sip on my wine again: this solitary ritual—the sacrament, the repeated libations of my new lifestyle—is just as comforting. Feeling a little mellow already, this current course of life seems pretty awesome to me. The constant flow of existence and the cycle I find myself trapped in don't bother me one bit.

I then remember my mother, her happy-sad eyes during our videoconference. I remember my younger brother's face, radiant with the promise of his upcoming college graduation, and the news I received about my youngest brother, his rise to rock stardom in our barrio. I remember the last time I saw them: the one was about five or six years old, the other no more than a toddler. The fact that they have a different father hasn't kept them from considering me their eldest brother. The absent brother. The one who lives on "the other side," the one they occasionally talk to on the phone, the one who has seen them grow up through the pictures they kept sending him in the mail.

The plight of the undocumented is no illusion: it is distance, clandestinity, criminalization, vulnerability, fear, lack of mobility, exclusion, uncertainty, humiliation.

But the United States has an inherent aversion to stories having to do with impossibility and frustration and sadness and won't allow them to take root on its turf. It is here that one of the most common platitudes uttered by politicians from either party about the issue of immigration acquires true significance: the United States is a country of laws, but it is also a compassionate nation. And so I might not be allowed to travel and be reunited with my family, but the United States and its compassionate genius (its technological wonders) won't deny me their presence.

When they miss their family, other people I know schedule a trip. I, a video chat.

TWO
OF THINGS LOST

My father lived a very short life. He died at the height of his youth, at twenty-two, just days after I was born. He was an artisan. Had I been more sensitive during my youth, I would have done everything to preserve the sun-shaped mirror he had crafted with his own hands. The mirror that hung, for an unexplainable reason, on a wall of my grandmother's patio. After my father's death, my mother and I went to live there. Until I was about fourteen, I saw the mirror hanging on the blue wall every time I went out onto the sunny patio. It was around that time that I started noticing that its colors were beginning to fade. After years of exposure to the generous sunlight of Guadalajara, the cheerful rainbow of flames shooting out of the rounded mirror was now beginning to lose its charm—the multicolor flames were now giving way to a taciturn autumn scene. Years of neglect had taken their toll on this intricate, colorful mirror that had probably been a gift to my mother. The mirror she had surely used when putting makeup on looking forward to seeing my father was now meeting its demise. Fourteen or fifteen years later, time had slowly nibbled away at it—two or three strings of rusty water rolled down the mirror, and dry leaves that once were blue, yellow, and green flames were now beginning to chip away.

This mirror was the only material possession I could have called an inheritance. But time, which takes away everything we are and do (Leopardi), and my own neglect robbed me of it.

The memories—or rather thoughts—I have of my father are few and widely scattered. My first memory of him is, obviously, his absence. One of my earliest recollections is that of running in front of the windows of a storefront that was a pharmacy and a clothing, shoe, and fabric store all at once. I remember running in front of the windows and seeing a little neighbor of mine walking hand in hand with his father. Back then, like now, I was very curious. Also back then, like now, I knew I should remain quiet. I saw little Manuel holding the hand of his father and felt like asking my mother, who was sitting on the step of the pharmacy, her chin resting on both her palms, her sad gaze fixed on the bell tower of our church, where my father was.

But I didn't.

A few years later, during my paternal grandmother's funeral when I was about six or seven, I remember standing right next to my mother as the grave diggers prepared my grandmother's final resting place. I remember, too, how their heads kept going lower and lower each time they produced a new shovel of dirt. And I, embracing my mother's legs, remember pile after pile of dirt coming out of the hole, out of the family burial site. Amid those piles, I saw a piece of mustard-color fabric and something that looked like a small elephant tusk—it was my father, tossed around indistinctly in a random shovel of dirt from below.

That was the first time I experienced the terror of life, as my mother let out the saddest cry I've ever heard. My mother cried and screamed aloud, but she kept enough strength to turn my gaze—like an American poet says—away from history and toward the place where all human aches begin. She didn't tell me what the reason for her sudden distress was. But back at my uncle's, I heard him say that he remembered that my father had been buried wearing a shirt that color.

Those remains—the yellow shirtsleeve, the lonely rib—were the closest I ever came to my father. And now, as I type these words, I wonder whether the grave diggers, with the hurried, relentless pace of their shovel blades, broke through my father's coffin.

Did you even have a coffin, Papá?

Back then, like now, I lacked the courage to ask my mother about my father, let alone about his death. I'm too much of a coward. But one day I will have to, I'm sure. One day I will have to settle matters within myself: know the exact date of his death, why he died, what his personality was like, what he liked doing. Of this, however, I am sure: that he was a man of a sensitive soul, for my mother preserved a notebook full of poems written by him for her. Early in my childhood, when I first attempted a few lines of my own, she was moved to tears, telling me that this inclination could not come from me, but must necessarily be an inherited one.

It occurs to me that I was not meant to be here, reflecting on my past, writing this confrontation, recording this coming to terms with myself. Now that I am familiar with the traditions and characters of different peoples, it also occurs to me that, by all spiritual affinity, I should have been born a Brit, so that I could proudly celebrate magnanimous Edinburgh without, or suffer foggy London within. I should've been born a late Greek, a Roman, an Indian so that I could have been schooled in the arts of the flesh, of stoicism and asceticism all at once. But instead, I was born a Mexican.

Being born poor and Mexican—that is the ridiculous sum of my personal tragedy.

My birth predetermined my future. Born a disadvantaged Mexican in the twentieth century, I inherited resignation, resentment, mistrust, social misery—all of which paved the way to my migration, to the contemplation of these thoughts. My past has brought me to this juncture where my greatest achievement has been becoming a translator of obscure documents no one will ever read, an undocumented Mexican immigrant surrounded by the ever-closing circle, by the ever-choking circle of American law that now lays its fingers upon my throat.

::::

More than thirty-six years have passed since my father's death, enough time for my mother to reconstruct her life. After many years, she remarried, had two more children. She's got her own house now. The house where I lived for a few years before making my way to the United States. A house that I distinctively remember as being only half built.

The last picture I received of my home back in Mexico came in a letter, when letters were still sent. The facade in the picture is painted burgundy and white. The fence—a tall and elegantly intricate construction crafted by a local artisan and handed down to my mother by her younger, better-off sister—is also white. On the left side of the house there is—a standard feature of Mexican homes—a *cochera,* the parking space that has always been empty at my mother's. To the right is the kitchen, and between the kitchen's window and the fence, there sits a modest but well-tended garden featuring a bush blooming with orange roses. The green of the grass and that of a tall pine tree—already reaching the half-built balcony when the picture was taken—stand in sharp contrast with the burgundy and white of the facade. The year I left for the States, I suggested to my *Jefa,* as I call her out of deference, that a small palm tree would look great in the middle of what still was a lifeless and arid spot reserved for the garden. But she planted this pine tree instead. In spite of that, the letter she wrote me years later was beautiful, and I felt her heart pouring out with best wishes and tears. She wanted to show me how the front of her house looked now that the first floor was all finished and painted and, especially, with a garden. Before my departure, the house was only halfway completed, the facade nothing more than a rustic brick wall and the garden an empty space. So seeing the front of her house painted and with a garden was a real delight. But what truly moved me was the last line of her letter, "Mi jardín está precioso, pero me faltas tú."

Many years have passed since I received that letter, and many more since I've been home. In spite of time and distance, my mother and I have been in close contact throughout the years. There was a period, however, during which this communication was awfully truncated. My mother fell—weightless—down the obscure jaws of a sadness no one around her ever understood.

During that period, I came upon an article that said that in previous centuries, those conspicuously withdrawn were thought of as either possessed or robbed of their souls. They were affected not only by their sickness but also by the chastisement of those around them. Even to date, lack of information about emotional illnesses is still rampant in the Mexico of my family.

Throughout the period of her sadness, my mother's siblings never stopped visiting her or taking her places. But they didn't grasp the seriousness of her condition. I eventually learned that, when visited or taken to someone else's house, she would sit quietly in a corner while my aunts and uncles ate, drank, and danced. Their little brigade of children would run wildly around my mother's chair. Noticing her petrified disposition, some pulled gently on her hair. Some of those little angels made faces at her; others mocked her.

Garrulous by nature, my mother became extremely quiet. And, thanks to it, I became a better listener. Unable to travel and be with her, I could do nothing else but phone her daily and listen to her silence. I learned that on days when I heard nothing other than her breathing, she was irremediably lost, roaming amid the dark corridors of some remote chamber of her being. When she sobbed quietly, however, I always felt the blade of a scalpel running down my chest, sensing that her distress was too great for me to even imagine, and would be simply impossible to bear.

But that's all over now. And painful as it was, my mother emerged from that dark retreat of hers with a sharper aesthetic sense. If her taste had been delicate beforehand, now it was nothing short of superb.

Years later I received an e-mail from one of my brothers with a link to a video he'd shot of the house and uploaded onto YouTube.

How different it looks now! The elegant but sober burgundy color has given way to a bright lime green. My mother tells me that, upon recovery, the first thing she asked for was that the facade of her house be painted green. A happy lime green that, according to some anthropologists, would have been one among the many bright colors of choice in the palette favored by ancient Mexicans.

When I say that the house underwent a transformation, what I mean is that my mother's healing process is reflected all throughout her home. It is a five-minute silent video—my mother is absent, the older of my two brothers says only a couple of words, while the younger one gives me the finger, and a punk song fades in the background within the first couple of minutes. The video reveals a house full of light, full of plants and flowers all around: in the kitchen, in the staircase to the second floor, in the living room, in the patio. But the healing is broader. It created a space for historical reconciliation. It healed not only my mother's emotional wounds—it cured the whole family of the prejudices congenital to the Mexican heart.

My mother imagined she was creating a decorated space whose beauty would soothe her. What she didn't know was that it would open its doors to a way of seeing ourselves. Coexistence. Before my departure to the States some seventeen years ago, my generation was infatuated with everything foreign. All things that came from abroad were highly valued among us. Which also meant that the local, especially the indigenous, was looked down upon. It was worthless. Our folklore was for tourists. We were cool, not exotic. All that was unworthy of us. A source of shame. Distancing ourselves from the manifestations of the local soul made us proud. And we believed showing it was our obligation. Everyone did it in their own visible way. I, for instance, ventured to plaster a Metallica poster on my bedroom wall. My mother frowned at it, unleashing a litany of disapproval. But she never dared take it down.

The preference for the foreign has not changed in current-day Mexico. What has changed is the appreciation for the local. Which brings me back to my mother's house.

Each of my brothers' bedrooms features the Mexican and the Latin American the same way they feature the American and the British. They all coexist within their walls. An image of Emiliano Zapata hangs right next to a poster of NOFX. El Che and an "Alto a las corridas de toros" poster are taped to a closet door. Unlike the uncomplicated *malinchismo* of my youth, my brothers' generation has produced more complex individuals. No longer embarrassed or stigmatized by their own background, they have embraced it. Their bedroom walls are a mosaic of ages and continents.

In the end, however, the great winner in the battle to occupy the salmon walls of my mother's house has been our indigenous past. What stands out throughout the walls of the first and second floors, in the living rooms of both floors, in the bedrooms themselves, is a presence felt through its colors: from the lime-green facade to the paintings that decorate the whole house, one can sense that a great domestic revolution has taken place there, and that this time it is the indigenous element that has been vindicated. Its stoicism has finally paid off. The radical quietism of the indigenous soul survived the humiliation, the loathing, and indifference of its own countrymen. Now it occupies a central place on my mother's walls.

They say that upon Constantine's conversion to Christianity, the Roman Empire also underwent a spiritual revolution. After centuries of vituperation and clandestinity, the followers of Jesus, the Christ, came out of their catacombs. The God of love, of compassion and redemption, was admitted in the pagan company of Venus, of Jupiter and Mars. The Christians had survived Nero, his irate reign. Some of their grandparents had been turned into human torches, illuminating the vast gardens of Caesar. Others (scores of them!) had been fed to the beasts in those very gardens, under the generous light produced by the burning bodies of their brethren. But things were bound to change. By the time of Constantine, the roles had been reversed. The Christians came down from the poles and whacked almighty Caesar's ass with them. Constantine, the man who would be god, now knelt before the bishops, listening devotedly to their admonitions. Rome was declining, and they were there to restore its moral life.

In Mexico something similar happened, except that—like all things Mexican—it happened backward. Whereas in Rome Christ was, as it were, promoted, in Mexico he has been gradually demoted. The Catholic padres neglected the lesson from their ancestors. They allowed a local cult to gain traction. A purely marginal and indigenous phenomenon upon her apparition, by now la Virgen de Guadalupe has claimed her rightful place among Mexicans. And one need not look too far for evidence. A simple instance from the video I received is living proof—a big, colorful painting of la Virgen hangs strategically placed right in the middle of my mother's bedroom, above the headboard of her bed. On one of her nightstands, the one to the right, there sits the image of the Santo Niño de Atocha, a minor god and performer of miracles. On the other, there is the figure of another adopted god: Jesus, the Christ. Just like Christ displaced the figure of Caesar and became the sole ruler of Rome, la Virgen to date has become the spiritual goddess of Mexico, displacing the figure of Christ to a lower level in our metaphysical affinity.

Toward the end of the video, I am left thinking that within my mother's house, great progress has been made. A change whose development I was unable to witness, except in this five-minute shoot that descended upon me like some distant but moving revelation. But whether the reality I have speculated about here is also true in the Mexico that lies beyond the walls of my mother's fortress, I do not know, as I am unable to witness it in person.

: : :

Also among the things I have lost over time is the private idyll of my childhood.

Every morning, carrying on a tradition started as an adolescent back home, I accompany my first cup of coffee with a piece of pastry from a Mexican bakery. *Una sema, una concha, un ojo de buey, un niño envuelto.* But my favorite by far is what they call a *magdalena,* which is nothing like its Spanish counterpart or what the French call madeleines. Which actually makes me think the lady at the bakery probably made the name up. When I asked her what the name of that pastry was, she looked confused and hesitated before answering. She then mumbled the name. Perhaps she found it embarrassing not knowing the names of each pastry sold there, and she simply blurted the first thing that popped in her head?

Be that as it may, starting my mornings with a hot cup of coffee and a *magdalena,* with its shredded toasted coconut spread evenly over the top and the raisins my teeth so eagerly dive after, preempts any and all minor calamities, any embarrassment awaiting me at work or in the city at large. Or the simple bitterness of being alive. And, when the bakery has run out of *magdalenas* on Monday nights when I usually stop by after work, well then I just get a week's supply of any other kind of pastry. Anything will do, as long as it helps me calm down the yearning. As long as it can appease this rowdy stomach that wakes me up growling in anticipation of that treat.

I've tried to convince myself that this morning craving has underlying reasons. Three main reasons. The first one being that my morning pastry is so delicious, even when the fruit plate sitting right next to it makes it look unhealthful. And second, because indulging in this little thirty-five-cent treat early in the morning creates the illusion that things will be just as good for the rest of the day. But in reality, the most deep-rooted reason I so adamantly follow this daily custom is that it keeps my memory alive.

It is like a habit I've inherited and was asked to keep. It has allowed me to keep certain regularity in my life, a homey tradition that remains unbroken even after being away from home for so long. I guess I ought to be grateful that fate brought me to Chicago, where Mexican bakeries are abundant and inexpensive. Bakeries I visit once a week so that I don't have to go back every day. Especially on cold mornings like this one, when people down at the bus stop shiver like wet little birds shaking off an excess of water.

Do they have any such consolation, those poor shivering souls bundled up, those souls braving the arctic cold of Chicago?

The coffee came only in my adolescence, but the bread has always been there, as far as I can remember. It is part of my earliest memories and definitely the first memory of my working life. I must have been about six or seven when, alongside the youngest of my maternal uncles, I started delivering pastries to our neighbors' doorsteps. He'd carry the tray, sometimes on his head, finding the perfect balance as he walked. Most times, however, he carried it on his broad right shoulder. And I, his sidekick, would walk along with him, highly satisfied by our labor. It made people happy. It made them smile and thank us profusely. The streets of our neighborhood, our commercial route, had something of an enchanted story about them. A fairy tale where the role of some children was to be children and play outside with their siblings and friends, while mine was to bring them the irreplaceable joy of pastries. As soon as they saw us approaching, me and my uncle, they'd rush over to meet us. Screaming, their eyes big and round, their mouths watering, they'd approach us, our little regulars. Then their mothers would come out of their houses shortly after to pay for their children's snacks.

I've worked a great number of odds jobs since then, many of which I've forgotten. But not those days. I have always cherished those memories of my childhood. Those evenings after school when the abundant sun of Guadalajara would begin to set in the horizon. It would sink behind the iconic yellow and blue twin towers of the city's *Catedral*. A sea of blues and purples and reds and oranges would soon devour it, and all of this was followed by the emerging darkness creeping up from Tonalá. Innocent of my economic disadvantage and not yet frustrated by my social condition, back then I saw life under a different light. The course of things seemed normal and natural. After all, just like my little neighbors, I'd also get to play outside. But only after all deliveries were made and we had returned the borrowed tray from Panadería Tokyo. Only after we had cashed in and brought our little share of income and left-over bread back home.

An even deeper memory of my childhood is related not to my native Guadalajara, but to my family's ancestral village in Zacatecas, where my great-grandparents lived and whom I remember visiting a few times during my childhood. They were both humble farmers, my great-grandparents, almost illiterate rural folk. There was something puzzling in their relationship to the earth. They lived inside that undulating, singing skirt made out of corn that Octavio Paz sang about, its rustle constantly serenading their ears. Perhaps because of their proximity to it, they didn't believe, as I do now, in the mythology of corn.

I believe in Centéotl, Lord of Corn. I believe that, upon birth, he buried himself in the ground so his semen would impregnate the earth. I believe this is whence we spring. I believe this is our true origin. I believe we Mexicans are made of corn. I believe in the sacredness of patience, in the collective effort of generations. I believe in every second invested over those thousands of years, in the prolonged observation, in the scientific study and examination. I believe in this wild grain destined to become nourishment and god of a people. I believe in the seen and unseen properties and virtues of this great human achievement. I believe the domestication of corn implies a pact that cannot be broken. I believe in this intimate covenant. I believe a kernel of corn constantly flourishes within me. I believe in the wisdom of the Popol Vuh, whose gods made a flawed man out of corn so he could worship, give thanks, offer tribute. I believe in this perfect circle. This subterranean grain that rises from the earth, reaches out, and offers its fruit to man. This nourishment. This prayer gracing the arid Mexican soil, making it a fertile bosom.

But neither Papá Santos nor Mamá Ramona romanticized corn. For them, corn was no poetry. In Papá Santos's hands, corn was as solid as the wooden yoke around his oxen's necks. Along with beans, it was the grain he grew in his fields. In Mamá Ramona's hands, corn was transformed—it became broken specks and dough. Simply ground, the corn grains fed the chickens, leaving the shaven cob to the pigs. Put through a different process, it fed her children.

In retrospect, I now begin to have only a vague hint of the invaluable lessons inherent in those childhood memories of my visits to them. Bean and corn fields, the mooing of cows and early rooster crowing. It was there that I was able to witness habits stretching back centuries, probably millennia. Like all country people, Papá

Santos rose at dawn and went about his business. He fed his poultry, milked his cows, picked beans from the fields. And even though our daily meals always varied, the central food, the one that was always present, was corn in the form of tortillas. A tortilla I always willingly ate and never thanked anyone for. A tortilla: the closing point of a perfect circle. The final product of a process that started in Papá Santos's callous hands plowing the soil, impregnating the earth with the kernel, and patiently tending to it until it was prime time for its picking. It was back then that I witnessed the dedicated labor of a man who, to quote Miguel Ángel Asturias, was "corn become man planter of corn."

The tortilla I ate was corn put through a highly complex process that involved some steps whose names sounded foreign and mysterious to me: *milpa, maíz, molino, cal, nixtamal, metate, masa, comal: tortilla*. It was in the generous, wrinkled hands of Mamá Ramona that this process came to an end. Happy to see her great-grandchildren sit at the table of her adobe kitchen, she never asked anyone for help. Never did she demand the strength of our young arms to chop the wood for the fire. Never did she tire of telling us stories while boiling the corn, making it into *masa* and shaping it into those circles that would, in some minutes, satisfy our hunger. No sooner had a steaming tortilla fallen into the *tortillero* than one of us sitting at the table reached out for it. Never did we truly see—anxious as were we to indulge in it—Mamá Ramona's royal table crowned with the miracle of corn made tortilla.

Now, decades later, every time I walk into a Mexican restaurant offering homemade tortillas, I can't help but feel both nostalgic and satisfied. In a bustling kitchen near my house, Doña Irene replicates Mamá Ramona's ritual. On the weekends, the restaurant is full of people, and each of the thirty-plus tables requires at least two orders of four tortillas—industrial quantities, considering the slow preparation pace. Still, Doña Irene tends punctually to each tortilla: she takes a ball of *masa*, flattens it with her heavy wooden press, picks up the raw dough disc, and lays it down on the flat grill. From a distance, her work has the monotony of an assembly line. Yet there must be an implicit mystery, some hidden joy in the slow, delicate manipulation of each tortilla. An air bubble raises slowly in the center of the tortilla, cueing her to flip it quickly. Her right hand obeys and moves with precision, while she smiles and hums the song oozing out of the speakers in the dinning room.

Is that a smile of gratitude or satisfaction? A memory of her own childhood? Like me, Doña Irene is most likely undocumented. But this doesn't seem to matter. After all, to adapt an ancient Roman saying, *Ubi panis ibi patria*: where there is corn, there is my home.

THREE
MY ADULT EDUCATION

English

When I arrived in Chicago, one of the first things that caught my attention was the absence of life out on the streets. Life in the United States, I would soon learn, is lived indoors. And it was there, secluded in the intimacy of distant relatives' houses, still bemused by the strange new world surrounding me, that I first glimpsed the complexity of language here in the States. I observed, for instance, that children spoke mostly English, while adults spoke exclusively Spanish. The fact that adults wouldn't answer in English to their children at first seemed something laudable, something that spoke well of them. I saw this as a perfectly normal way of helping children preserve the language of their parents. After all, I had no doubt that, had they wanted, my relatives could have replied to their children in their new language. I had naively assumed that all of my relatives living in Chicago must have learned English already. After all, many of them had been here for more than twenty or thirty years. But that assumption was about to be proved wrong.

Just a few weeks after arriving in Chicago, I moved into my cousin Pedro's house. One Saturday he invited me to the mall. Eight years my senior, Pedro has a beautiful family. Along with us came his little five-year-old girl. I remember thinking that he had probably brought her along to buy her a little doll. However, despite her repeated angelic requests and an eventual tantrum, Pedro stood his ground. She would have no such thing. Heading to the shoe store, his reason for bringing her along became clear. She'd be our interpreter. After trying on some shoes too big for him, he told her to go ask the salesman for a pair in a smaller size. And off she went, little Norma, with her TV-learned English, to comply with her father's request.

Witnessing my cousin's complacency and his total dependence on his child was a decisive moment in my life in the United States. It made me feel embarrassed and afraid at the same time. What if fate had something similar in store for me? The very thought frightened me.

Pedro's reasons for not learning English intrigued me. I never asked him, but gave it much thought on my own. Maybe he never had the opportunity to learn it, I'd tell myself. Or maybe he'd been working a lot since he first came (about nine years before me) and he simply hadn't had enough time to sign up for classes.

I lived at Pedro's for a few months, working along with him and other relatives at a factory for a few weeks. It was then that I realized it wasn't the case that he didn't have enough time to learn English. He lacked the will. He simply didn't care. He was uninterested in the world beyond the factory line. He found fulfillment in the obscenities of the Mexican radio hosts he listened to at work, in his armchair conveniently placed right in front of the television set that was always tuned to the Spanish channels.

In the next chapter, I will write about my slow and ongoing process of learning the complicated nuances of the English language, especially spoken English. I will also write about the complications this created in my relationship with my relatives. For now, let it suffice to say that the behavior I observed in my surroundings in my early life in Chicago was crucial in my decision to start learning English immediately.

It wasn't long after my trip to the mall with Pedro and his daughter that I learned about a community college close to his house where

CHAPTER THREE

English classes were offered for free. After learning this, I switched jobs right away. I left the coveted morning shift at the factory and went to work as a dishwasher at a Mexican restaurant. I'd be working evenings, and this would allow me to go to ESL (English as a second language) classes during the day.

I completed the five levels of ESL in two years. I embarked on the learning of English hoping to ease my way into a community I looked forward to joining. I wanted to conduct myself in society with the liberty of a native speaker. I had grown up watching Hollywood movies, and, once living in Chicago, listening to spoken English in person made me wish to speak it even more. I wanted its agility, its wit.

Learning English also offered me immediate rewards. It allowed me, for instance, to resume my education.

Many years before, my formal education had been cut short because I didn't pass the entrance exam at the *prepa* (high school equivalent, which the generosity of Mexican politicians will make mandatory beginning in 2022) in my native Guadalajara. When I learned I had not gotten in, I was disappointed, but it was a buffered disappointment. Since early in my childhood, I had learned to equate school with adversity, in terms of both access and performance. School was not in my genes. It was not for me.

Even if I had passed the entrance exam, chances are I would have dropped out shortly after. The economic situation of my family was such that I couldn't afford to finish. Like millions of Mexican teenagers, one of my obligations was to bring home my little share of income so my family could make ends meet.

But I had a consolation. I was the first person in my immediate family's history to ever take the *prepa* entrance exam. That was my accomplishment, and I took great pride in it.

Upon entering the American education system, I was placed in the high school dropout category. Paradoxically, considering that 50 percent of Mexicans haven't completed grammar school, receiving too little education carries a profound stigma among us, and my case was no exception. Being aware of this made me feel ashamed. Going forward in my life in the United States, I imagined my whole moral character would be judged on my lack of education alone. So embarrassed and afraid was I about this that whenever my relatives drove me around the south suburbs of Chicago filling out applications at factories, stopping by at construction sites to see if they needed an extra set of young arms, or at restaurant kitchens to ask whether they needed a dishwasher, I'd put down on the application that I had completed high school. But I lied. It was not until I started taking ESL classes that I found out I could study for the GED and get my high school equivalency diploma.

After one and a half years of English lessons, I took the GED test for the first time and failed it. Then I went back to my books, studied every morning before my English lessons and every evening after work, took the test over, and failed it again. It was only on the third try that I was able to pass it. Having done this, I thought of myself as an accomplished, intelligent man. I was satisfied and happy with myself.

I received my GED diploma shortly after, and I was sure I was through with school. All my relatives and coworkers were in awe. They celebrated my achievement. They were utterly convinced that, with the coveted diploma, the doors of prosperity would be thrown open for me. When I left South Suburban College, I did so with the illusion of finding a decent job. But the next five years found me still washing dishes and performing a number of odd jobs.

Then it occurred to me that I should probably apply for college. What did I have to lose? I applied to another community college. When I received the acceptance letter, I quit the last of the odd jobs I'd been holding during those five years and decided to keep working at the Mexican restaurant only. That evening I put on my long, waterproof vinyl apron and a hairnet, and I continued my dishwashing activities. Somehow, these wages would get me through college.

After taking the GED test three times, I had gotten a glimpse of just how ill prepared I was for the challenge of higher education. But I had also learned something about myself: that, regardless of how difficult it might be, given the opportunity, I could rise to the occasion. Every day for the next six years of college and grad school, I dedicated all of my time exclusively to two activities: work and study. In the evenings, I would work at the restaurant and then go home and do home-work—the easier assignments—tackling the most difficult readings with a fresh head early in the mornings before going to class. I lacked preparation and language skills, but my hope was that my will and discipline would make up for that. And it was with this determination and the invaluable instruction of teachers like Ms. Hill-Matula, my reading-skills professor to whom I am deeply indebted, that I began my first year as a college student, taking basic reading, arithmetic, ge-ography, and an introduction to philosophy class.

Moraine Valley

Sitting in a classroom full of people some ten years my junior, I was immediately dazed, confused, and blinded by the light of Plato's al-legory. It was my first encounter with philosophy. I *am* like one of those people in the cave, I remember telling myself while sitting at my desk, mesmerized. I felt a metal ring pressing around my ankles and the weight of invisible chains binding me to the darkness.

My bewilderment followed me for months outside the classroom, and it was such that, while at work, I felt that my obligation as a thinking being was to question the motives of the cooks when they demanded that I hurry up with the plates. Ha! As though my quicker scrubbing would make any difference in the great scheme of things! Didn't they know that the essence of things was permanent and un-changeable? That motion is an impossibility because between one point and another, there is always a middle point, and from that middle point to another point, there are an infinite number of middle points? "Tran-quilos," I felt like saying, "we're not gonna get anywhere; you're all being deceived by your senses." Or should I simply comply with their urgent request and remain aloof and unaffected? A different theory, that of Heraclitus, assured me that the person they were screaming at earlier and the one doing the thinking were two completely different people. I felt compelled to engage the cooks in Socratic dialogue to try to prove whether the plates they demanded were actually what they thought them to be or if they'd been living in a lie all along. Chained in the cave, they were being fooled by shadows. An idea like that would certainly confound them! But then, guessing their reply, "¡Déjate de chingaderas y apúrate con esos pinches platos!" I dropped the pursuit of my philosophical inquiries and scrubbed the plates harder.

The treasures of the English language and literature and philosophy worked their wonders on me, but with unpleasant results. I ventured into that vast universe a naive, optimistic young person, only to be spun out of it years later a confused, bitter, and resentful man. What was I, a dishwasher, doing reading about the apotheosis of John Milton's Satan? What was I doing exploring the dark chambers of Hamlet's thought? Why did I have to delve into the American virtue of self-sufficiency, the faith to impose one's will over the challenges of life preached by Ralph Waldo Emerson? What business did I have reading about the ravages of Nietzsche's blond beast when I myself was a ravaged beast of burden?

I don't know the answer to any these questions, except to say that such readings were an early part of my adult education, of the awakening of a sensibility, of the discovery of a fantastic realm, a distant dimension unknown to me until I was about twenty-eight years of age.

Thus, wrapped in a cloud of mysteries, I passed my first two years of college. Before completing my associate's degree at Moraine Valley, I was summoned to a meeting with my academic adviser. There I was told that I should start planning to attend a four-year college. There were applications to fill out, scholarships to apply for.

Being the first one in my family to go to college, I had no example to follow. This made things relatively easy because I had nothing to prove to anyone, nothing to live up to, and this gave me great liberty. But it also left me at such a loss that when my adviser asked me what I wanted to major in, I immediately blurted, "Philosophy!" And that was that. He didn't question me. Didn't oppose my choice. Busy as he was, he started browsing the Internet for some programs in the area I could apply to.

If I were to identify the moments that determined my life afterward, this brief interview with my adviser would be one of them. Yes, I made a choice, but I wasn't offered any options. I wasn't told, for instance, that a bachelor's degree in philosophy wouldn't get me a job; I wasn't told that I was limiting my employment opportunities; I wasn't told that maybe I should consider other more marketable professions, like accounting or business administration. This, I realize now, would have changed my life. It would have offered me the opportunity for a career that would pay off, a practical way of overcoming my socioeconomic disadvantage.

Now, many years after the fact, I regard it as a great irony that the poor advice I received resulted in my getting a first-rate liberal education. This, of course, was at the expense of faster social mobility. However, the decision I made regarding my education was the purest choice I could have made. It was influenced neither by greed nor by any other pecuniary consideration. My desire rose out of the barbarous impulse George Santayana deems necessary for all passionate reveries. A great awakening had occurred in me during my first philosophy lesson, and I meant to live it to the fullest.

After an agonizing wait of a couple of months, I started receiving letters from the colleges I had applied to. Because my only ambition was to continue studying philosophy and apparently the demand for that major was rather low, I was accepted to all programs I applied to. But only one offered me a scholarship. And this, being offered a scholarship, was highly encouraging and a huge relief. Unable to apply for state or federal financial aid, I had been paying the full amount of my tuition on my own. Luckily by then, I'd been promoted at work. After a year or so of college, my English and my education had helped me make my way out of the kitchen and into the dining room of the restaurant where I worked. I was offered a job as a busboy and a barback, which I immediately accepted and took great pride in. And this was a promotion indeed: the job wasn't as hard, the servers were much nicer than the cooks, my hourly wage went up by a dollar, and, most important, I started receiving tips every night. This helped me pay for my tuition and gave me the idea that I was well on my way to prosperity.

Things went like this for my remaining semester at the community college. School expenses and supplies were part of my education, and I worked hard to meet these financial obligations. The long and painful mornings, nights, and weekends studying physics, trigonometry, and calculus I simply saw as a productive way of investing my time, even if I wasn't producing anything other than mere intellectual stimulus. And, when overwhelmed by the nature of acceleration and the calculation of derivatives, I often found myself escaping on a mental flight, reflecting on the fact that I had made some real progress since my first days of ESL some seven years earlier. My economic situation might not have improved a lot since then, but inside me a silent revolution was beginning to stir.

Lake Forest College

Driving for the first time through the streets of Lake Forest, I was in awe of what I saw. This suburban community was like a magical forest village where order, cleanliness, and visible wealth contrasted sharply with the chaos, filth, and poverty of the Mexican neighborhood I'd driven from just an hour earlier. The first thing that drew my attention in this Chicago suburb was its symmetry, its order, its civility.

During the time I had lived in Chicago, I had been to many other suburbs, but none compared to this one. Its boundless wealth transpired from its winding, stony streets, from the architecture of its old mansions, from its downtown shops. But that was only the prelude to what awaited me. Lake Forest College was the most beautiful school I had ever seen. It seduced me with its secluded charm, with its vast forest preserve, its trees towering way above, crowning my experience that cool and cloudy afternoon. As I was early for my appointment, I walked through the campus in a daze, feeling transported to a different dimension, fantasizing about just how wonderful, how perfect, it would be to devote myself to the study of philosophy while immersed in such a place. How many mysteries would reveal themselves to me during my eventual morning walks through those enchanted woods? The gray skies of that afternoon gave me the illusion that there was a German air to the campus, and this, I was sure, would help me untangle the theories of Leibniz, Wolff, Kant, Hegel, Schopenhauer, Heidegger.

Just a couple of weeks earlier, I had received a letter from the admissions office. In an effort to recruit minorities, Lake Forest College had offered me a scholarship. I received the letter and read it almost in ecstasy, barely believing my eyes. My adviser had suggested that I apply there, saying that it was a nice small liberal arts college. What I did not know about liberal arts colleges was that they were out of my league, impossible for me to afford. But I was not discouraged, and for a time I entertained the illusion that I could pull it off, the exorbitant tuition. The scholarship I was offered covered only half the tuition total, leaving me to pay the other half plus room and board, the grand total of which was much more than I could afford.

But that didn't matter. I conceived plans: I'd do both, work and go to school full-time. I had done that successfully for the past two years. Because the money I'd make wouldn't be enough, I'd ask a relative to lend me some, promising to pay him back quickly after graduation. I had heard that most college students have tremendous student loans to pay after graduating, and I assumed I would be in debt too. Given my circumstances, it would probably take much longer for me to pay it off, but I didn't care. What I cared about was that I was on my way to prosperity. At least in appearance.

Who would have thought that I, an undocumented immigrant who not so long before was still washing dishes for a living, would now be rubbing shoulders with rich kids from all over the country? Perhaps that was my real break, my opportunity to meet someone there, a businessperson who would see my potential and offer me the opportunity I so coveted.

In the end, however, I wound up not attending Lake Forest College. I went to my appointment, was given a tour of the campus, and as we were walking through the buildings, as I was introduced to the different student-body organizations and fraternities, I realized that I didn't belong there. The more I witnessed the boundless wealth, the more I saw it pour copiously from the halls, from the dorms, from the student lounges, the more acutely aware I became of my own destitution, of the vast ocean that separated me from everyone else there. I tried to ignore this, and even for a couple of weeks after my appointment I tried to convince myself that I could do it. But the truth had already anchored me to my concrete reality, and I ended up attending a state university instead.

UIC

One of the letters of acceptance I received came from the University of Illinois at Chicago. They didn't offer me any scholarships, but the incentive to continue my education was there. Even though UIC lacked the charm of Lake Forest College—which my naïveté equated with quality of education—I was glad to have been accepted. Going to an aesthetically pleasing school had been my ambition, as though allure could compensate for substance—how Mexican of me!

UIC may not have fulfilled my cosmetic demands, but having been accepted boosted my confidence. It gave me a sense of accomplishment. Having settled for it, I attended the orientation session.

As soon as I arrived on campus, I recognized the surroundings. I remembered that many years before, just a few weeks after arriving in Chicago, I had once passed by the Halsted main entrance. I was in a landscaping truck. Sandwiched between my cousin and our American boss, we were on our way to mow some rich person's lawn. Without any prospect of ever attending college myself, I watched the hordes of students coming in and out of the main building. They walked in a hurry in front of us, their backpacks full of promise, of knowledge. As we sat in the truck waiting for the traffic light to turn green, I was assailed by different emotions—I felt secretly embarrassed and angry, excited and hopeful. Two worlds were crossing paths, the one inside the truck and the one outside. I belonged to the former. I did not belong in the cool shade of the classroom, in the comfort of study halls, in the discussions in the conference rooms, or in the sacred silence of the library—those places were definitely not for me.

I belonged out in the open. My work was physical rather than mental. My brotherhood was with the massive lawn mower. Under the oppressive heat of the approaching summer, man and machine were fated to become one. We'd fall into perfect step. A harmonic dance at the rhythm of the engine's noise as I hurriedly paced after it. A dance driven by the scent of burning gas, freshly cut grass, and the intense summer humidity that would give me a heat rash, making my whole body itch and burn.

Still, I sat there, watching mesmerized. That world in front of me seemed so distant. So foreign was the spectacle unfolding in front of me that the students themselves seemed like a different species altogether. What was I, a poor Mexican, doing so close to the United States and so far from God?

Now, on my way to orientation, I found myself crossing the very same street I had once driven by, re-creating a scene of many years past, but from a different perspective. The world I had felt excluded from now opened its doors and welcomed me and made me feel important. Privileged. Gone were the days of toil and strenuous physical labor. I was now ready and fully determined to show everyone my potential. Mind you—I didn't know who "everyone" was or what my alleged "potential" was. In fact, now that I think of it, what made me proud was the sheer *idea* of attending college rather than any eventual success. I had no clue what I'd end up doing after graduation, for my understanding of a college education was ideological rather than pragmatic.

Ever since I had sat in my first philosophy class two years earlier, I had passionately cherished and secretly advanced the notion that an educated man, if he were to be so truly, should cultivate his intellect rather than attend to the economic demands imposed on him by the world. The nourishment of the mind must take precedence over the concrete banality of daily life. Thus spoke my dogmatic self.

Blinded by the light emanating from Plato's cave, I held dear to my principles. My faith in the life of the mind remained impervious. And so began my junior year as a philosophy student.

At UIC my zeal increased in direct proportion to the intensity of the light shed on me. Every day I was bombarded with new and exciting ideas: Leibniz impressed me with his boundless imagination, with the variety, the vastness, and the scientific precision of his fantastic universe. I was fascinated by Descartes's method, by his novelty. Hume shocked me with his irreverence, seduced me with his prose, and captivated me with the rigor of his intellect. And the genius of

Königsberg, Immanuel Kant, tore me apart with his contemplative dialectic between the stars and the soul.

So effective was my education that by the end of my senior year, I was ready to graduate with a firm standing in philosophy but with no clue whatsoever about what to do with my life thereafter. My life had been transformed—I had undergone a silent revolution so private in nature that it left no visible scars other than a paradoxical and growing stigma.

Upon graduation, I realized that my devoted and intense years of study had turned me into an utterly useless member of society.

But I learned my lesson—immediately after graduating, I began a master's in Latin American literature at the same university. During my college years, I never took any related classes, so applying to the program was simply a hopeful attempt to find something worthwhile to do after graduation. When I received the letter welcoming me to the program, I decided to attend, perhaps in an effort to prolong the impending confrontation with reality outside school. I was happy to keep working at the restaurant, having been promoted to bartender and waiter over time. My tips were enough to cover my expenses, and I was starting to take an interest in some Latin American authors.

Needless to say, prior to my enrollment in the master's program, my exposure to the literary tradition of Latin America had basically been nonexistent. I grew up in a house where the only book to be found was a dusty Bible no one ever read and that was always kept—like some sacred ornament—behind a well-lit and spotless glass cabinet. My family's reading material basically consisted of copious weekly comics. Hence, I never acquired the habit of reading. And, not having made it into *prepa,* I didn't really have a chance to develop that habit on my own.

The two years of my master's went by rather quickly, and toward the end of the program I felt I still hadn't had enough time to familiarize myself with the entire Latin American tradition. More than thirty-one years old at the time, I also felt I had to take my future more seriously. I thought it was time to change gears and transfer my skills from serving tables to a more useful enterprise. Because, if

I am to be honest, up until then, the philosophy and literature books I studied in college had only messed with my head—they had gotten me into trouble, both with myself and with others around me. I had truly believed in Baltasar Gracián's idea that only culture can redeem man from the bestial. But in my case, my newly acquired cultural understanding wasn't proving itself good for much.

: : :

About a year after I graduated from the master's program, a law was enacted making it possible for undocumented immigrants to attend public colleges in Illinois paying in-state tuition. Compared with the exorbitant fees undocumented students had to pay before, this was a huge break. Before, tuition for the undocumented had been the same as that charged to foreign students. The difference was, of course, that the undocumented did not have rich parents in foreign countries to pay for them.

Over the three years following my graduation from my bachelor's, I had repeatedly run into former classmates I had studied philosophy with. Talking to them, I found out that none had pursued philosophy at the graduate level. A bachelor's degree in philosophy, I found, is merely a springboard to prepare you in the rigor of logical thinking, in the elaboration of sound arguments and the recognition of flawed reasoning. Many of my former classmates had chosen philosophy as a way to prepare themselves for medical school and law school.

Gradually, I realized the fool I had made of myself by pursing a master's in literature. So when I read in the papers about the new law for immigrants, I felt that a great opportunity was opening on the horizon.

I Dream

The realization I came to was that, if I were to really do something with my life, I should go into a profitable career. But my ambition was even greater than this—I would be the quintessential American success story, the immigrant who came from nothing and reached the top in spite of all odds. By any standards, I had come a long way already: I had gone through ESL and gotten my GED in a little more than two years after arriving in Chicago; eventually, I put myself through college and grad school. This was more than I ever expected. Yet I was not satisfied, and I felt a drive, an ambition, to keep climbing the ladder of success. Except that this time I had *really* learned my lesson. I would not allow ideology to get in the way of concrete gain. This time my goal was clear—I'd study law.

The Illinois in-state tuition law for undocumented students was enacted, and, a year later, I was already engaged in the application process. I had researched the state schools I could attend, and I was aware of the costs and had saved enough to cover the expenses of the first year of law school. I had also signed up for an LSAT preparation course and dedicated hours every day and whole weekends to studying the books and doing the exercises online. More important, I made sure that, if I passed the test and did everything right, I would be formally accepted. I e-mailed the entrance coordinator and explained my situation. The secretary was nice and helpful. She told me that, indeed, the new tuition law also applied to law school. I shouldn't have any problems applying and getting accepted.

Everything seemed to be going well, and the time to take the LSAT was approaching. Weeks and months went by, and I looked forward to the day with expectation and optimism. The classroom lessons and the book strategies made a lot of sense, and my timing and scores kept improving. But then an unexpected formality got in my way. It was a requirement that all LSAT takers provide an identification card and their Social Security number and have their pictures taken. The company in charge of administering the test would keep this information permanently in their database. What, I wondered, if they not only kept it but actually did a background check? What would happen if I was caught trying to use a fake Social Security number to take an entrance test into a field whose very nature excluded me?

I then realized the highly paradoxical nature of my endeavor. Just as I had many years earlier, I was again trying to sneak into a space whose main rule was my exclusion. My clandestine crossing of the border had delivered me safely to the gates of economic solvency and to the path to self-fulfillment. But my mobility was limited. The liberty I had found was merely an illusion. To quote a popular Mexican song, my situation was—and is—a "golden cage" wherein my flight was nothing but a prolonged dream. Had I made it into law school, I would have become a prisoner devoted to studying the shiny walls of his incarceration. Boethius's Wheel of Fortune kept spinning around its eternal cycles, and I was caught in them. I had hopped on it the first day of my college life. It had been a joyful and upward ride. By preparing for law school, I had reached the summit of my cycle, and now its natural descent began.

With the consolation of avoiding years of silent humiliation, I logged off the LSAT website. I took my books and shelved them away. And with this, my dream of reaching the heights of success and my secret desire to speak with the eloquence of the courts were also put to rest.

FOUR
THE SONG OF THE CICADAS

Ask any undocumented driver what, on a regular workday, he fears most. He will likely tell you he is afraid of being pulled over. After work the shadow of illegality creeps out of factories and kitchens and rides on highways.

I, however, was spared this risk for a good number of years.

As I have written in earlier chapters, a few months after arriving in Chicago, I wove myself into the dark workings of the Illinois secretary of state. A legal driver's license and state ID were the first significant purchase of my life in the United States. They required almost two months' salary. But that didn't matter. It was a long-term investment that began to pay for itself almost immediately.

The lights of the patrol car flash in my rearview mirror. I pull over. This is my first encounter with an American police officer since I have been rambling loosely in this limbo of my semilegality. I have just gotten my driver's license. I touch my right pocket and feel my wallet. Its contents give me a great sense of confidence. A sensation that borders on impunity. For months my wallet has been (and will continue to be) pretty much empty. Most of my wages go toward paying for my smuggling, my identification cards, and the old car I have just bought from a relative for four hundred dollars. I have not been able to save any money, but my recent investment is about to yield its first dividends.

In just a moment, I'll reach for my driver's license and hand it to the police officer. I'll set the crooked gears of the secretary of state in motion. The cycle of bribery will have come full circle. For now I sit quietly, waiting for the officer. I put on a broad smile.

Never have I felt so much at ease before the law.

My license and registration check out. I already know why Officer Grand stopped me and have plans of fixing the problem over the weekend. However, as I have just recently started ESL classes, *turn signal* is a term I still don't know. So, when he asks whether I know why he pulled me over, I say, "Jes, da *directionals* no work."

Officer Grand smiles. He says, kindly, "I'm sorry?" Excited about the opportunity to continue practicing my English, I repeat myself, nodding confidently, "Jes, jes, da *directionals* estop of work."

He looks confused and shakes his head gently. He hints at me to repeat myself. In a hesitant and lower voice, I say, "My directionals . . ."

Officer Grand can't make out my jumbled speech. He is getting frustrated. I repeat myself in several other ways I think appropriate. His face begins to transform. He becomes visibly impatient. Looks irritated. His body stiffens.

I now know it is time to stop. My futile attempt has annoyed him. Officer Grand frowns. He asks, "Do you even speak English?"

It is an early Friday morning, and I do not get a ticket. I am allowed to go with just a verbal warning. I feel humiliated. My face feels warm. I look in the mirror—it is red with embarrassment.

Soon after, I arrive at my ESL class, where I refuse to speak English all day.

The Language of Possibility

Learning English has been the great challenge of my adult life.

An undocumented immigrant, my irregular status should be my main concern. And it is indeed a most onerous burden. Were it only up to me, I would have dispelled this dark cloud looming over me a long time ago. But, over time, there is nothing a man can't get used to, and the gray horizon of illegality is no exception. I have learned to keep it at bay by lying, by ducking, by pretending it does not exist, and finally by disappearing into the shady corridors of clandestinity.

But my inability to communicate properly, clearly, and successfully cannot be hidden. This faltering tongue, this succession of mispronounced words, is what engages me continuously. What concerns me minute by minute is not what I can hide but how I present myself.

I often envy other people's ease at navigating the tides of daily life, however turbulent. It is in those moments that I most painfully realize how much a fair fluency of *spoken* English would benefit me. It would lessen the embarrassment of my inability to communicate well. It would draw away unwanted attention. It would relieve me of this feeling of homelessness that unsettles me.

I am walking the streets of downtown Chicago. I carry myself with the confident gait of a middle-class man. A disheveled-looking guy about my age approaches me. He asks me for a dollar. With agile language, he explains to me the reasons for his request. I mistrust him. Such joviality, such energy, such trendiness, so much theatricality, the obvious strength of his four intact limbs. There is something wicked in his appeal for charity. But his speech is colorful and happy, convincing and cohesive. The way he expresses himself makes him fully credible and persuasive. His spoken language is pure genius.

As he parts from me, I am left envying him, the unwavering confidence of his cool urban lexicon.

One of the disadvantages of learning a language as an adult is that one's tongue has stiffened. The mastery of a new language requires an elastic tongue, a responsive and lively tongue. And mine is now robotic and languid. At twenty years of age, when I began to study English, my vocal habits were already formed. The new prospect was exciting, but for a tongue accustomed to an ebb and flow from different depths, the twists and swirls of a new language were and still are overwhelming challenges.

In my new language, my tongue stumbles. I utter screeching noises. No matter how much I might love the English language—its guttural sounds, the biting of the lower lip, the buzzing sound, the vibration of the tongue, the oral wealth that pours like honey out of others—all that has proven to be beyond my linguistic abilities. And the fact that I can complain about it in writing brings no consolation.

: : :

Until I came to the United States, language to me had never implied a problem. Quite the contrary, growing up poor and uncouth in Mexico, I was never silenced. The imaginative colloquialism of the language I spoke served to express the frustrations, the helplessness of those like myself. But it always did so playfully. This is the true genius of the Mexican language of my childhood—that it always found charm in misery, a way to turn economic oppression into a laughing matter.

The great success of the alchemists at Mexico's television giant, Televisa—that fantastic realm of the imagination—was to turn economic misery into gold. They dissected the tragedy of the Mexican poor and fed it back to us as romance and parody. And it was in this symbiotic relationship that I was nourished. The wit I learned in my childhood was stewed and seasoned to perfection in the cauldrons of San Ángel and Churubusco, where Televisa's headquarters are located.

But it was only out in real life that it soared to its proper height. During my childhood, it always seemed to me that the irreverence and disobedience of TV antiheroes had a lot of catching up to do. Their wit echoed and bounced off the living-room walls of every Mexican household. But the *astucia* of the Chespirito characters barely compared to the witticisms of some people I knew. They were my neighbors, my classmates, my relatives whose lives unfolded on the stage of the barrio streets where I lived.

Their craft consisted of confusing and outsmarting their opponents. They knitted dark webs around their victims and then attacked them. Known as *albur,* the game consisted of an intricate fusion of insult and pun, meant to show off one's cunning. This was the preeminent element of the language of my youth, an idiosyncrasy of the Mexican tongue. It was its charm. Its beauty. It was the challenge posed to the other in order to confuse him, to outsmart him, to obtain a sense of achievement when looking at his perplexed face as he tried to untangle the web that had just been woven around him. Building one's reputation as a daring and respectable *alburero* was the highest distinction one could obtain in the poverty-ridden neighborhood where I grew up. And, even if I had nothing else, at least the malleable language of my youth always offered me that possibility.

I never became a master *alburero*, however. My relationship to my language never reached those heights where imagination soars and spreads its wings in full liberty. Rather, I limited myself to listening and to keeping from getting drawn into an *albur* challenge, from which I could only come out embarrassed. Still, the dark codes of Mexican colloquial language were not unknown to me. I had developed such an intimacy with them that I knew just how to use them to express my resentment, my disapproval of and rejection toward authority in particular and society in general.

An unemployed young adult with no prospect of pursuing higher education, I barely had any need to express myself otherwise. Thus, when the time came, I made my way northward with nothing more than an irreverent tongue and a two-thousand-dollar debt for my smuggling.

::::

Upon arriving in the United States, I was immediately seduced by what seemed to be unlimited wealth. The serpentine shape of the highways. The huge, verdant suburban lawns. The glaring shopping malls. The skyscrapers. The enthusiasm and productivity of the people.

Here all things spoke differently—they spoke the language of possibility. I now found myself in the land of plenty where achievement was within my reach. The contrast with the place I had come from was so sharp that, to allude to Arthur Schopenhauer, this new world had the air of an idea. And, removed as I was from it because of the language barrier, it remained an abstraction, but I *willed* to make it part of my concrete reality.

Perhaps because of our proximity to wealth, the contrast I saw between the way my relatives in Chicago lived and the world that surrounded us was startling. At my relatives' homes, the echoes of poverty, resignation, and apathy that were so familiar back in Mexico here seemed to be amplified. It was as though the whole of Mexico had multiplied and landed squarely there, on the kitchen table, in the living room, in the mold-smelling basement bedroom where I slept. Mexico oozed out of the radio and the television. It spoke to us in her comforting maternal tongue. And, when we most needed to be awake, her tender voice lulled us back to sleep.

Thus, I found myself transported to a different country but without really living in it, without participating in its life. It was like I never left Mexico. Rather, it seemed as though I had traveled deeper inside instead.

Because I was fully dependent on my relatives who had no interest in American life, I found myself isolated, stranded, unmotivated. Whoever got the idea of identifying foreigners with the label of "alien resident" knew exactly what he was doing. A green card may grant you legal status, but it doesn't take away the stigma of alienation. It doesn't guarantee your integration in society.

Lacking both the assurance of legality and the benefit of integration, I was overcome by a deep feeling of unease. Only a few weeks before, tunneling under a high, rusty iron wall, I had crawled across the border and sneaked into clandestinity. But now the challenge before me was of a different nature. Already inside the walls of empire, I was free to walk in broad daylight. But like Droctulft, the barbarian, I went about my new home without understanding a word, unable to decipher its symbols, dazzled by its imposing presence, by its complex and shiny verticality.

Upon crossing the border, I discovered that the place I found excluded me. Like the flaming sword of the scriptures, the local tongue was the sentinel that kept me at bay.

Yanko Goorall

Without a good grasp of English, I was nothing but a bundle of flesh and bone still waiting for the breath of life. I only half existed. My effect on others was no greater than that of a cabinet, a stop sign, a park bench. I was voiceless in my new home, but I might as well had been unborn.

Thus, out of a pressing need to exist, I realized, in a very Cartesian fashion, that first I must learn to speak, and only then could I be.

In his inquiry into the origin of language, Charles Darwin concludes that the first humans to use it employed it in courting females, seducing them for reproduction. If that was the case, then I was more than happy to court the English language, to coo and dance around it until I could possess it. My new language, I reasoned, would guide me out of obscurity. It would be a torch leading me out of the shadows of anonymity and onto broad daylight.

It took me about two years to make my way through the complete offering of ESL courses at South Suburban College. However, outside of class activities, I barely had a chance to practice my spoken English. Most of my classmates were Spanish speakers, and, since none of us were confident or advanced enough in our new language, we inevitably reverted back to Spanish every time we got a chance.

The situation at work and at home was even less conducive to practicing my new language. Surrounded by Mexicans in both places, I soon became their favorite object of mockery. In their opinion, mine was a useless endeavor. All the English I needed was that which could help me get by on a day-to-day basis. If I was to learn it, then I should do it in this pragmatic fashion. Trying to learn it well was a waste of time. We had all come here to work, and I ought to be grateful and take that opportunity more seriously.

Role models abounded. Some of my cousins and coworkers around my age were getting married. Some had children already. A few among them were buying their own houses.

Prosperity. The unsought advice kept coming. I should take a second job at another restaurant, just like the rest of my colleagues at the kitchen where I worked. Or, my relatives insisted, I should go back to the factory and try to get back that "great job" I was so lucky to find shortly after arriving in Chicago and I'd so rashly quit in order to start ESL classes.

Work- and family-oriented folk, their comments were always well intended. In their minds, my desire to study English thoroughly was an eccentric and reckless decision, nothing more than a quixotic endeavor. By pursuing it, I showed great irresponsibility, immaturity, and disregard for the truly important aspects of life. I should focus on my concrete needs. I had a family back in Mexico who could use all the help they could get from me. Every penny I could earn scrubbing dishes, mowing lawns, or at the assembly line. Plus, they were quick to remind me, I still owed most of the money I had borrowed to pay for the bus from Guadalajara to Tijuana, the meals, the phone calls, the hotel, the coyote who smuggled me, the plane ticket from Los Angeles to Chicago.

These were some of their honest observations. In their opinion, my idea was a luxury beyond the means of a working-class Mexican immigrant. I often found myself wondering whether investing so much time learning English was the wisest decision as well. Shouldn't I stop playing Mr. Smart? Wasn't it pointless to pursue a goal that was doomed from the beginning? Wasn't it absurd for me to try to wake up a dusty brain? In order to improve my situation, wasn't it easier just to deploy the full strength of my young muscle? Who did I think I was, trying to break away from the traditional role of the Mexican migrant worker? Wasn't I fooling myself? Wasn't this all just a spectacle? Wasn't I faithfully embracing an endemic Mexican vice—the vice of appearances? Who was I trying to impress and why? In the end, wasn't it all a futile chase after the wind?

Not having a definite answer to these questions stirred a great uneasiness in me. When I considered them, all these worries felt like a blade severing the ties that bonded me to those who had welcomed me in their home in a time of great need.

Thus, my first years in the United States were a constant struggle not only with the language I wished to learn, but also with my surroundings. With my whole background.

In the end, my family members were largely right. Almost seventeen years later, I still haven't mastered spoken English completely. My conversations with native speakers immediately reveal my shortcomings, my flaws, my distortion of their language. In their puzzled faces, in their frowning, I can still see Officer Grand's fading image. I notice my lack of diction in the way they lean toward me to better hear me.

Like the character in Joseph Conrad's story, when I speak English, even the most familiar words acquire a peculiar intonation, as though they were words of an unearthly language.

Thus, amid much confusion and disapproval regarding my decision to learn English well, only one thing was sufficiently clear—I had become a problem to myself.

Broken Spanish

The television is on. It is many years later, and Michelle Obama is delivering her memorable speech at the Democratic National Convention. Her speech is highly emotional, especially as she paints a tender portrait of her working-class father. Both our fathers are a common detail in our biographies, and this moves me deeply. I feel a subterranean connection, a common bond with the future first lady. As she speaks of her father's illness and how, in spite of his deteriorating health, he continued to work diligently for the City of Chicago, her speech reaches its emotional climax. The camera scans the crowd, and I discover other people sobbing and weeping as well.

I sip on my wine, on this solace. Already on my third glass this Monday night, it is easy enough for me to blame my sensibility on the bottle to my left. Thinking about the story I've just heard, I remember some stories I grew up hearing—the lives of the people around me were just as moving. If nothing else, the lives of working-class folk are rich in drama and tragedy.

If it isn't her story per se that moves me, what is it then? Mrs. Obama goes on with her speech, perfectly enunciating each word, elevating the pitch of her voice to create greater impact, pausing a second or two after a shocking statement, contemplating a point on the horizon, above the heads of the crowd, nodding lightly, like approving the work and actions of her deceased father, and then resuming her narrative. Such skill.

It is the inherent spell in the nature of her speech—the perfect mix of eloquence and wisdom that Cicero praises—that hypnotizes me.

That and the wine, the memories of a father I never met, and the political content of the speech I just heard.

: : :

Fluent spoken language is a skill I have been gradually losing. By learning English thoroughly, my hope was to be fully functional in both communities. As time went by, however, a rift started to draw me away not only from those around me but also from myself. More and more, I began noticing it, the distance, the isolation. The person I was upon leaving my native city started to become a stranger.

I am speaking to my mother on the phone. She sounds confused. Asks me to pause and explain myself over: *A ver, dímelo otra vez, hijo.* Again. My young brothers find it intriguing. They tease me. They are convinced that my broken Spanish is inversely proportional to my fluency in English. They ask me to sound out English words for them. I please them. WOW! They wish they could speak it too!

I hang up, go downstairs to the convenience store, and ask the cashier where to find a particular kind of toothpaste. He smiles kindly. He lowers his face and asks, "Sorry. Say that again?"

Over the years, coherent spoken language has become increasingly foreign to me. Quiet by nature, whenever I have a chance to speak, I am now capable only of delivering a short string of loosely related thoughts. Chopped-up sentences constructed with ill-chosen and mispronounced words. I might have never been one of the most daring *albureros* in the Guadalajara of my youth, but at least back then I knew where I stood, and the ground was firm and familiar. Never during my youth did I feel ambivalent about the use of language. I spoke the Spanish of the masses, the Spanish of the Mexican working class, the Spanish of my family. And though I did not know it then, this provided me with a sense of security and comfort. I belonged to a community whose language was as clear as the skies that graced it.

It was not until I ventured into the study of English that my Spanish began to suffer. Its magic began to dwindle, and my speaking ability began a slow but steady decline. What once was an agile part of me began losing steam. And as my contact with the homeland became more and more sporadic, as the rift that separated me from my relatives in Chicago became wider, and as my solitude grew, my native spoken language experienced a premature and melancholy withering. It had been transplanted into a foreign soil, and now it became this dying thing. This thing vying to survive. Like sad autumn leaves, I had been slowly shedding fragments of my mother tongue over the cycles of my life away from home. In a process parallel to my own, my spoken language lost its youthful spirit. Over a matter of years, I went from possessing a colorful, vibrant, and solid language to having nothing more than the remnants of it, a rudimentary instrument of communication. Its ruins. The sad reminder of better times gone by.

Mainly out of fear of acknowledging it, I managed to ignore my problems with my spoken Spanish for a long time. But then it gradually became clear—I was unable to transfer thought to word. Slowly, with each bit of English I acquired, I began losing the capacity to articulate complex thoughts in my mother tongue. I spoke in broad terms, but the crucial skill of detailed conversation had slipped out of my brain.

I'd be around others and hear them explain things. They'd talk about simple and complicated matters, sprinkling their explanations with color and detail and colloquial expressions that at some point had been well known to me but that now sounded strange and novel. And it seemed to me that speaking like them, with confidence and ease, was the most natural thing in the world. Something wonderful. Something so effortless it required no thinking. Their speech flowed so spontaneously and it was so vibrant it embarrassed me. The fact that I had once communicated just as well, so freely and easily, that once I'd been the possessor of such a lively and colorful tongue saddened me.

The wealth of Mexican colloquial language had been the one aspect of my culture I felt truly proud of growing up, and now I listened to it like a foreigner listens to a new language. The ties that bound me to my background had been gradually loosening their grip on me, deteriorating slowly until I felt quite embarrassed at my lack of articulation, diction, and ability to sustain prolonged conversations.

A linguistic cripple, I grew quieter. I assumed a somber disposition. Some relatives I still visited at times thought it had finally caught up with me, my illegality. They thought that all the years away from my family were finally taking their toll on me, and that the long separation from them was responsible for this silence that drowned me. They worried. They'd see me drinking quietly at their gatherings and feared I would become like one of those guys roaming the alleys—a Mexican immigrant who, instead of dreams, had found fulfillment in a permanent and pleasant state of inebriation.

It wasn't that I didn't want to speak. I had simply lost my confidence in doing it. More frequently than I was willing to admit, I found myself lacking the ability to utter a coherent response to a situation I was enthusiastic about. I found myself gesticulating more than I used to, nodding, expressing my full approval with expressions like "¡Órale!" and "¡No, pos tá chingón!" Or, when I felt strongly against a matter at hand and it merited a full-hearted response, I'd simply drop my head backward and slightly to the left, opening my mouth widely and uttering expressions like "¡Chale!" and "¡Que no se pasen de lanzas!" with which I exhausted the limits of my eloquence.

During my reveries about my new language, I had envisioned a collision of two brandishing tongues. But they never collided, never came close to each other. Rather, they receded indifferently from one another, leaving me there, stuttering. Without a firm footing in either of these two languages, the most essential of human ties was severed, and I felt like an orphan. A living proof of William Gass's assertion that the language of the poor is as lousy as their lives.

If it is true, as Jean-Paul Sartre says, that the language we speak is the mirror of our world, then mine at the time was rather foggy and crooked, for the images it reflected were quite nebulous and distorted. Without realizing it for years, I had been gradually slipping down the slopes of a linguistic limbo I had not foreseen.

The Tongue That Vilifies Me

When I first made the pilgrimage northward in search of prosperity, it never crossed my mind that learning a new language would be such a challenge, such a high hurdle to overcome, such a powerful force to contend with. The first few years of learning were particularly difficult, as they confronted me with myself and revealed my lack of preparation, my numerous limitations. My mind was baffled, and I found myself roaming about in the midst of a hazy limbo, finding comfort in neither Spanish nor English. But then, after a prolonged period of confusion, the haze began to clear, and I started making my way out of that dark pit.

I owe my awakening to reading. An unprecedented activity in my life, the seemingly innocuous act of reading shook me with the violence of an earthquake. Reading messed with my head. It turned my world upside down. Specifically, I am indebted to a handful of books I came across when I first started college. And even though I can't pretend I fully understood them at the time, the narratives they contained unleashed in me the ability to dream that for so long had lain dormant. I was taking leave of one stage of my life and entering another. As I continued learning English, I started to develop the habit of reading. It was a slower but parallel process, and the better understanding I had of my new language, the more intense my passion for reading grew. It was an activity that came to placate the inner convulsions I'd been going through for years.

I read philosophy. The *Discourses* of Epictetus and his inherent endurance and abnegation immediately appealed to me, to my current situation. But that philosophy seemed so distant it could not be applied to the circumstances that surrounded me. Or so I reasoned until I read the narrative of Frederick Douglass. I then understood that Epictetus's thought was not dead. Its virtues were not some curious relic, some museum parchment. They were something very much alive and closer to home than I imagined.

Douglass embodied the virtues of stoicism, while at the same time—and with a strength of spirit uniquely American—he negated and rejected its fatalism. Through the painstaking effort of teaching himself to read and write, Douglass learned the redeeming nature of language, and this allowed him to decode the scheme that kept him in bondage. Of his message, I heard only the distant echo of the prophet. But it was enough to whisper confidence into my confused soul to help me break free from what I considered my own bondage. Sartre was right—literature does throw you into a battle, and the battle I waged was that of my own redemption.

Everything I had lost externally over the years started to be compensated internally. I realized that language served several purposes and traveled through different channels. The wounded pride of my inability to communicate well with others began healing when I started listening to myself more carefully.

Though still bound to the dishwasher at the restaurant where I worked, something in me had broken free. I was free of its scorching steam, free of the pots and pans piling up around me, free of my menial occupation, free of pressures, free of the cooks yelling as they demanded more plates, "¡En chinga, cabrón!"

Something similar happened when I discovered the sacred wisdom of the Hindu scriptures. But those mysterious books, too, were in need of a more contemporary American rendition. It was Henry David Thoreau who, lying quietly by his pond, interpreted for me the exquisitely mystical secrets of that remote universe.

I might have occupied the lowest rung in the employee hierarchy of the restaurant where I worked at the time, and I might have been relegated to the back of the kitchen, but inside my head I was slowly becoming a man of the world. A seed of cosmopolitanism was beginning to blossom in my spirit. I was now beginning to crave my own voice. Reading the essays of Ralph Waldo Emerson gave me the boldness, the confidence, needed to believe that one day this plate-scrubbing business could be transformed and take on poetic forms. I dreamed of one day telling my own story.

: : :

The desire to record my experience was as genuine as it was puzzling. I must have been driven by that demon George Orwell writes about, which one can neither resist nor understand. After all, it was one thing for me to feel a need to relate my experience, but to do it in English? I needed to tell my story, and what better way to engage in this bitter solace of writing than by first confronting and then fully embracing this tongue that rejects me, the tongue used daily to demean me and vilify me?

The choice was also practical. Of the two languages I could only half express myself in at the time, it was English that offered me greater liberty. That might seem odd. An exaggeration. But to understand my conundrum with language, you'd have to consider the circumstances that have surrounded me.

My formal education in Spanish had stopped when I was about thirteen years of age. Therefore, I first learned to read and analyze texts, to write and formulate abstract thought, in English. But this happened only at about twenty-eight years old, when I started college. In my basic reading-skills class, I was taught how to identify tones of voice, make inferences, and understand plots. The process engaged me thoroughly, and the mystery of language began unfolding as I started putting elaborate sentences together, developing ideas, strengthening arguments. Soon I was writing whole papers, analyzing an essay about a story I had just read, dissecting its argument, *refuting* its premise!

That was a deeply rewarding experience. One that made me feel important. It was as though I were the sole constructor of a tower I both built and climbed at the same time. A tower that provided me with an increasingly clear and broad view, for it rose out of the depths I had been driven to by my circumstances. It led me out of that foggy territory I had started to wander in since the beginning of my incursion into English. Now, instead of the feeling of defeat that had dragged me down, I was being driven upward by a true belief in achievement. I was being propelled, as it were, by a renewed spirit. I was on my way to becoming the new bilingual person I'd so long dreamed about.

All of this happened during my college years, but only through a thorough and prolonged immersion into reading. That's how I began to have a better and more sophisticated understanding of my new language. But between the new and exciting reading and writing skills I was acquiring and those I'd learned as a child, there was a fifteen-year gap of obscurity and lack of use. A valley of darkness down which the light of the written word had ceased to shine.

: : :

Now, many years later, I feel free to execute this newly acquired habit of writing with the confidence and carelessness of a beginner. My amateur writing provides me with the perfect outlet to review my past and transform it.

Last year I read about a symposium on the crossing of the border, real or imaginary. A topic I am fully familiar with. One I have tried my own hands and knees at. It would take place at UIC, my alma mater. Some months before, I had written a few pages about the subject, so I submitted them.

My paper was accepted, and I was invited to participate. I, the most inept of men when it comes to public speaking; I, whose speaking process consists of a confused fluctuation between a deficient English and an ever-fading Spanish; *I* was being invited to read a paper at a symposium!

The situation was so ironic, I felt ridiculous. It is one thing for me to sit here and type my worries away, quite another to get up in front of an audience and deliver a speech in a language in which I feel utterly incompetent.

I considered the possibility of presenting my paper. My story would probably be one of the most genuine ones at the symposium. I might not use elaborate charts and fancy projectors to aid in the telling of my story. I might not possess the erudition of the professors who would speak and among whose data I'd most likely be nothing more than a number, a statistic. My talk would be based on experience. In my accented English, I would speak of the hardships of crossing and the lies that have secured my survival afterward.

By speaking of the writing of those pages and how it provided me with much-needed relief, I would deliver them a few drops of that chemical method Joseph Addison writes about. They would know of my intoxication, the major catharsis the writing of those pages provided me.

CHAPTER FOUR

However, remembering my thick accent, I realized it would be too distracting for the audience to focus on my story, so I declined the invitation. And that was the end of my little reverie.

The Mariachi's Trumpet

Every now and then, I still remember Officer Grand's frustration, his lesson. Ever since my encounter with him, the way I sound to others has been quite important to me. I have taken a particular interest in my accent because of its prominence and self-importance. No sooner do I open my mouth than it pops up with arrogance, with impunity.

My accent has a life of its own; it dwells in its own dimension; it is language raised to the second power, a magic wand that bestows charms or flaws where none exists. It incites the rage of the bitter, summons the curiosity of the friendly, courts the paternalism of the activist, provokes the mockery of your own kin.

For this I am greatly indebted to Officer Grand, who made me so self-conscious. The morning he pulled me over, I became fully aware of my identity as an other. It was the dawn of my alienation, the first glimpse of the unbridgeable abyss that separated me from the community I sought to be a part of.

I frequently remember his facial expressions, his reddened face, his puffy cheeks, his eyes filled with anger, his unapologetic demeanor. Many years have passed, and now it also occurs to me that maybe the way he treated me was no exception. After all, I was nothing special to him. Had he known me in my full capacity as a reliable dishwasher and an enthusiastic English learner at the time, he probably wouldn't have had anything against me. The wise Seneca would have advised him to resist the germs of anger, but Officer Grand was too busy paying heed to his instinct to have any time for philosophical reflection.

No, his anger couldn't be personal. His problem was with that which I represented. In his mind, *accent* and *doomsday* had similar meanings. And, like politics, all accents are local.

Surely, Officer Grand had been noticing it for years, our intrusion. He probably saw us Mexicans as prowlers, inching our way into his community, his schools, his churches, his hospitals, demanding services in our own language, taking the jobs that rightfully belonged to his neighbors.

In his mind, his monolingual community was under siege, and our encounter provided him with an opportunity to confront one of the agents of that irruption. This was his one chance to stop the dreaded advance of the Trojan burrito Richard Rodriguez writes about. He probably would have been glad to scare it away. Send it back in full retreat. He would have gladly hauled it away in his patrol car. But that was beyond his power and jurisdiction. What he *could* do was teach it its place, make it feel uncomfortable, unwelcome, pull down tightly on the bridle. Hush it.

That would be sufficiently satisfying. He'd been preparing to vent his frustration on someone, and the seeds of racism and bigotry that had probably been lying dormant in his heart for a long time blossomed wildly with the cool dew of that early Friday morning.

Or was it just a bad hangover, Officer Grand?

Whatever the case, this much is true: unlike many advocates for immigrant rights I'd eventually come across, Officer Grand was not paternalistic. He might not have liked my accent, but he prompted me to action. Although his intention was to humiliate me, I now see him in a different light and think of him as a good instructor. His standards were high, and his demand that I speak clearly was not unjust, only premature.

Now that I contemplate it from a considerable distance, his intolerance implied opportunity. Thanks to Officer Grand, a reality that otherwise would have remained hidden from me became crystal clear. And, contrary to what he might have intended, his attitude was kindness in disguise. His intention was to intimidate me, but his challenge made me self-conscious of my spoken deficiencies, of the long strides I'd have to take, the long distance I'd have to travel.

Over the years, I have come across others who, though with a different intention, have been eager to remind me of my accent. But, unlike Officer Grand, they have been enthusiastic and condescending and paternalistic. What Officer Grand found revolting, they have found fascinating.

There are a lot more Hispanophiles than I thought, and some of them find me exotic. A word, a phrase, a conversation piques their attention. Many a time, I've been approached by people wanting to practice their Spanish. They try a word or two. The bold attempt at a whole conversation. They approach me in the friendliest of ways. They seek to uncover my real voice, the voice that hides underneath this charade of mine, this distortion of their language. Their hope is to engage me, to uncover and hear the real me. Because—of this they're positive—my *true* voice must be sweeter, smoother, more mysterious than this borrowed tongue I find myself struggling with. This tongue I am trying to untangle. The nature of my voice, they imagine, is enigmatic. They wish to share my tongue, to possess it. They imagine their membership amid a congregation of dancing flames: an electric current that sparks in the brain, a secret urge that burns at the tip of the tongue, a sudden combustion that blazes down the bloodstream, the mariachi trumpet echoing, exploding like a tumultuous fiesta in the lower chambers of the heart.

: : :

I am now in my seventeenth year as a learner of English. My accent has improved somehow. Because I don't consider it as prominent anymore, my fear of embarrassment has also diminished. During the past five or six years, I have also made it a point to recover the full strength of my Spanish. Years of intense work have made me a more confident user of language. I now read, write, and speak in both languages. Depending on the context, I have the option of choosing what language to speak. With my bilingual coworkers, for instance, I usually opt for Spanish. It is less stressful. The sound of it is more natural to me. Of course, my conversations with them are full of Anglicisms, or tainted with an occasional syntax error, or distorted by minor mispronunciations. But these are some of the trade-offs I've made along the way. I've made some gains in my new language and suffered losses in my native tongue. But feeling that this shadow, this accent that's followed me around for years, is not as dark any more is a relief that reinvigorates my spirit and gives me the confidence to converse equally in both languages.

This afternoon, going through my e-mails, I find one by Ramón, whom I have just been talking to at lunch. He's just gotten back from his parents' estate in Michoacán. The pictures he showed us during lunch were amazing—a succession of green rolling hills, valleys graced with a mysterious and glorious early-morning mist. The figure of a local peasant with a huge basket of corncobs hanging on his back disappears into that mist. "¡Qué hermoso!" someone sitting at the table said, praising the picture. Ramón smiled proudly and agreed, "Sí, la verdad que sí."

His e-mail says he wants to tell me something about a project. I pick up the phone and dial his extension. Speaking to him in English, I start explaining that his new deadline may conflict with other things pending. Ramón seems puzzled:

"José . . . ?"

"Yes."

Then he bursts the bubble. Chuckling, he says:

"Dude, you sound *SOOO* nasal!"

Ramón doesn't actually strike the final blow. He keeps himself from adding, ". . . in English!" But I get it. The thorough mastery of spoken English I thought I'd achieved is still a long way off.

But since all I care about now is making things a bit easier, I make a smooth and resigned transition to Spanish. Switching mental gears, I say, "Ramón, leí tu correo sobre tal proyecto . . ."

As he explains the reasons for pushing back the deadline and his voice becomes a mere background noise, someone comes into the office to use the phone in the cubicle right next to mine. Right behind her, two other office mates enter the office, chatting about their plans for the weekend. The office is suddenly filled with lively conversation and laughs—the crisp sound of perfectly enunciated English! I keep hearing Ramón, but I no longer listen.

I find myself thinking of the fabled ass that hangs around, looking up at the same tree day after day, secretly wishing to sing along with the cicadas, hoping to join in their melodic chorus only to realize that all he can do is bray.

FIVE
AT WORK

Browsing the Internet, I read the headlines: Arizona passes law criminalizing every undocumented immigrant within its state boundaries. Last year, I read that a great number of undocumented workers in the American Apparel factory in Los Angeles had been fired. In Georgia a poultry plant was raided; the number arrested and eventually deported was close to two hundred. Last year, also, I read that the City of San Francisco—following the example set by New Haven—had decided to provide official IDs to its undocumented residents.

About two or three years ago, I read a story of an undocumented man crossing the border and finding a car that had been in an accident. The driver was dead, but her child had survived. Jorge R. had left his hometown in search of the American Dream. Smuggling himself across the desert, he had walked right into a nightmare. He gained the child's trust. He consoled him and stayed with him until help arrived. Whether this accidental hero was rewarded or simply handcuffed and taken back to the border is a sequel I did not catch.

For more than four years now, I have been punctually following the attempts to reform the immigration system. From the birth of the Kennedy-McCain bill to its demise at the clapping hands of House Republicans, I have seen the hopes of millions of people rise and fall, undulating with the tides of opinion polls and the future of political careers.

I finish reading the Arizona article. Another episode of the drama is over when I quit the Internet browser. I unfold my legs. Rolling my chair back, I sigh quietly. Sitting right here at my office desk, that depressing world seems to be taking place in a remote dimension. It unfolds behind my computer screen, beyond the length of the Internet cords that quench my morbid thirst. It is a world so alien to me, it makes the whole mess seem quite ludicrous.

Yet it isn't.

That I can sit at my desk at work and reflect thus is the greatest irony of my adult life—the paradox of an undocumented professional.

The paradox of my situation manifests itself acutely at certain times. For instance, I am often required to interview candidates vying for a position similar to my own. I dress up for the occasion. Wear a tie. Shave.

I read their resumé, greet them, see their faces, question them.

Their future hinges heavily on the impression I receive of them in the next twenty minutes. Our interview decides in part whether our paths will cross again.

I am asked to judge their qualifications. Yet during such interviews, the thought that assaults me is of a different nature. The Catholic sense of guilt of my childhood hasn't quite lost its grasp on my throat: shouldn't this middle-age man sitting right across from me, with all his experience and legal documents, be offered the job that I have sequestered? Or have I simply bought too much into their idea? The idea that portrays me as a lesser being, a trespasser, a criminal, someone who has no right to employment?

The doubts that assail me in private are the indisputable triumph of the conservative agenda, the same agenda that preaches free enterprise and turns the other way once its effects, like the displacement of people or mass migrations, become apparent. But reminding the United States of its contradictions is a pointless effort.

Almost a hundred years ago, during the East St. Louis riots, W. E. B. Du Bois observed that the human problems of its new residents who had recently come from the South were of no concern to that industrial city, so long as its grocers and saloon keepers flourished and its industries steamed and screamed and smoked and its bankers grew rich. Similarly, the immigration rallies of 2006 and 2010 in Chicago had no impact on the fat cats of LaSalle Street; they did not disturb the peaceful Sunday strolls of the residents of the Gold Coast; they did not find sympathy among the gentlemen at city hall, so we all just went back to work as usual, for Chicago still needs its toilets scrubbed, its tables wiped down.

Walking down the hall after the interview, I find myself engaged in this sort of thinking. I am debating whether I am violating some ethical principle. I wonder whether I should quit immediately and be at peace with my conscience when a group of Mexican janitors—energetic, jovial, and cracking obscure jokes at each other—happens by on their way to start their shift. It then becomes clear—a position like theirs would suit me better. It would be more in accord with my background.

The janitors disappear around the corner and into the changing room. I fix my tie and feel nostalgic. The pangs and joys of physical labor, how I miss them!

Listening to my *paisas*, I feel a yearning for my former life. I think of my first twelve years in Chicago. I think of my numerous occupations. The mowing of lawns that began early on those summer mornings. I remember those mornings and afternoons that seemed to stretch endlessly. The mugginess radiating from the unrelenting sun that never failed to give me a heat rash on my back, on my legs and arms, between my buttocks . . . I think of the equally oppressive temperature of the assembly line. There, a red-hot river of melted iron flowed right by my feet. And I think of the third and final ring of that hell so my own: the dishwasher station in the Mexican restaurant where I worked for more than twelve years. In spite of the never-ending succession of bins filled with dirty dishes, how fun it was! How fun to feel the adrenaline rushing through my veins, the pressure of the cooks yelling, "¡Platos, más platos!"

How secretive and exciting it was to steal a minute or two from my busyness to alleviate that awful heat rash! Among stocks of meats, fries, bottles of frozen strawberries, and more, the arctic climate of the walk-in freezer always offered a soothing embrace. In winter I would simply step outside and let my skin chill for a minute before returning to my station.

And then the *albur,* the vulgar game every Mexican male always engages in. The phallic and testicular allusions that the ever-active imagination of the Mexican male extends and multiplies to infinity. The chorizo, the chiles—jalapeño, poblano, ancho, the avocados, any given piece of raw meat—they are all soon endowed with sexual attributes as the cooks use them to aggressively joke with each other in a locker-room display betraying both Greek sensual innocence and Catholic sexual repression.

And then every other Friday night when John, the American bartender who insisted on being called Juan, brought back a couple of pitchers of beer to the kitchen. It can't get any better than this, I remember thinking: free beer and six dollars an hour! That's probably why I was the first one to thank John, "¡Gracias por las chelas, Juan!"

I truly meant it, since it was only Juan and, occasionally, Drew, one of the owners, who ever motivated us after a busy night. The other owner, Roberto, a man who came from my own city, never gave us anything. Instead, he was always on top of us, "¡Muevan la nalga cabrones que no tenemos toda la noche!"

And then there was the memorable day I got promoted from the kitchen to the restaurant floor. How different things looked there! Going from the kitchen to the restaurant was like entering a different dimension altogether. Although each table had a candle constantly burning in its center, the lighting in the dining room was much dimmer, the atmosphere more intimate. But it was also much louder. The door dividing the kitchen and the dining room reminded me of the tall rusty wall at the border I sneaked under—a piece of metal dividing two utterly different worlds.

It was then that my exposure to the parallel universe of American culture began, as I worked side by side with bartenders and waitresses. Those were certainly very happy years of my life!

And now, back at my current job, watching my *paisas* down the hall on their way to start their shift, I find comfort in the fact that during those years, I was less stigmatized. I was a happier person, a livelier man. Straying away from one's own kin, it seems, is to die a little, and the agony deepens in proportion to the distance taken. Back then I might have been well aware of my socioeconomic disadvantage, but I was utterly oblivious to my legal status. I was less troubled by questions of ethics, of right, of professionalism, less tortured by questions of justice and fairness, all too complicated for my mind to untangle.

: : :

The ways in which I have dealt with my undocumented status have evolved over time. During my years at the restaurant, I embraced a brazen approach. But upon landing my current job, I soon learned it was best to cast down my eyes.

At the restaurant, everyone knew that everyone else was undocumented, and thus there was nothing to hide. The same way my co-workers at the restaurant had no reason to think that any of us had legal papers, at my current job no one would suspect that an undocumented lurks among them.

Just the other day, during a break at work, I read an article about a Mexican activist here in Chicago. In it he denounced the Arizona law that was then being debated. He is an American citizen now. But, he is very proud to say, once he too was undocumented. He had now crossed the golden arches of the North. Now his outlook of life is vertical and promising.

I envied him. His confidence. His enthusiasm. His optimism. The heroic gesture of his activism. The triumphal finale of his provincial saga.

Then I thought of me, of my situation, of my own outlook on life, and it was circular and barren.

There is no heroism in clandestinity. There is only the hunt, the continual chase. There is only the inevitable: the humiliation, the lies, the silent confrontation, the daily battle, this overwhelming feeling of orphanhood you swallow quietly and in private.

And so I have been living it, this silent drama of mine. Thanks to my current job, over a period of almost five years I have climbed out of my disadvantaged background and reached the coveted American Dream. And by doing so, as though once wasn't enough, I have become invisible a second time.

Now I am a sneaky shadow wandering about in the fairyland of the American middle class. I have mastered the art of elusiveness. I have learned both to operate under the radar and to be alert at once.

Before, when the news of a deportation was the subject of conversation with my peers at the restaurant, I reacted instinctively and with indignation. Now, whenever someone in the office mentions anything related to undocumented immigration, I reply with cool commiseration.

Browsing the news, one of the secretaries asks me, "Did you see, José? They caught a group of forty-three people with fake documents working at an airport in Virginia."

I put on a sad face. I shake my head slowly and answer, "Pobre gente."

Slightly uncomfortable conversations such as these demand no more than a deep breath, acting normal, seeming unconcerned. More potentially dangerous situations, however, call for subtler strategies. One thing I have learned since I got this job is to withdraw, when needed, into secrecy, into silence.

One day during election season, Jorge, sitting right next to me, asks me if I watched the debate last night. I answer, "Yes! It was interesting!" Nadine walks into the office and joins in the conversation. She has made up her mind and will be voting for Obama.

Jorge has some concerns. He thinks McCain looked too old. The dude's gonna drop dead one of these days, he says. Rachel, who has been listening quietly, says she does not really like Obama, but she has no other choice. She would have gladly voted for Hillary, just to keep seeing Bill on the screen. But Obama she just does not like. Plain and simple.

As I sit there listening to their discussion, I start tracing back in my mind every single conversation I have had with each of them regarding my legal status. I have told Jorge the bureaucracy was overwhelming and that I'm simply not interested in American citizenship. But haven't I told Rachel that I am in the process of applying? And what about Nadine, what kind of nonsense have I told her? Such inconsistencies!

I feel time running out on me. When my turn comes to answer who I'll be voting for, I'll have to draw a friendly smile and utter another white lie. I'll have to carefully redirect the conversation topic. Or I'll have to spin my chair around and act as though I am typing an e-mail, dialing a number. In the worst of cases, I'll have to step out of the office. Go to the bathroom. To the cafeteria. Act as though I am mailing something to someone. But that will be too abrupt and will look suspicious.

I remain seated, listening to the details that have persuaded them. And then, after going round and round my head conceiving an exit strategy, weaving lies together, a small miracle happens. Satisfied that their votes will be cast for the right candidate for the right reasons, Nadine and Jorge return to their work stations. Equally satisfied with her choice, Rachel steps out of the office.

Only I am left staring down at the carpet in the center of the office. Though astonished and incredulous, I am glad that this time I did not have to lie. No explanation, no reasons were asked of me. I had anticipated a potential nailing to the cross of my illegality, but it came to naught.

In this uncertain world I inhabit, at least one thing is true—none of these three suspects anything about me.

After years of dodging questions, of taking cover, of fending myself, sometimes with elaborate lies and other times simply withdrawing into a deep silence, this moment provides me with a strange peace of mind, a strange sense of security I am not used to.

Perhaps this is what it means to be legal, finding protection behind this emotional barrier, behind the invisible shield of normality?

: : :

I often wonder how it will all go down. At first everything was threatening, even the mail I received from work. Every letter could spell trouble. Could that envelope be asking me to clarify the problem with my Social Security number? Or simply hearing my phone ring: could it be human resources, demanding that I show up there immediately? Or perhaps they'd bypass all diplomacy and send security directly to my cubicle to escort me out of the office? It would be almost comical, the way they'd find me: my earplugs on, enraptured in the parallel universe of music, my only consolation at the time.

Those were the scenarios that haunted me. The materialization of any one of them would mean the end of my little fantasy. But weeks, then months, and then years have gone by, and, perhaps because my life up until now has been so empty, I've come to appreciate it, the suspense, the latent threat, the thick air of this limbo.

: : :

Living in the shadows has its advantages. Years of physical labor and stigma (suspicious eyes fixed upon you like a puritan index finger) acquaint you well with the core virtues of stoicism. You also learn valuable lessons on skepticism. Thus, during moments like this one, I am well aware that the comfort of my air-conditioned office could be ephemeral and that at any second I could be forced out to work again under the scorching summer sun.

Over the course of my clandestine life, I have learned to see success and survival as synonyms. The one is performed in public, the other executed in the shadows. In my quest for survival, I've resorted to cunning, to hiding. A constant fugitive, I take shelter in the lofty flight of imagination.

Once, in Chicago, I was an American.

That day, like a bat, I flew by night. My transmutation, my naturalization, took flight in the dark, on election day. That day American citizenship would have redeemed me. I vote, therefore I exist—that would have been my maxim. My reality, however, is otherwise—I vote not, hence I exist not. Though a concrete part of a transnational problem, I am nothing more than a political ghost.

The scene takes place on election day. I show up to work early. I plan to keep to myself all day: finish all my pending work, clean my mailbox, answer e-mails, do anything to give the impression of being extremely busy and unable to leave my cubicle.

I am the first one to arrive in the office. I sit down at my desk, put my earplugs in, and pretend to be completely absorbed in my work. This way no one around me will bother me. They all know better than to disturb a hardworking man!

The first two hours go as planned, except that I realize I forgot to put my lunch in the fridge. I take a trip to the kitchenette and run into two coworkers chatting down the hall. One of them inquires whether I've voted already,

"NO!"

They giggle. Then they mock me, "NO!" one of them echoes with a deep voice.

I leave my lunch in the fridge and go back. I check my pager as I go past them again, pretending to be reading a page I never got.

Back at the office, Carla has just arrived. She is taking off her light-green jacket, which features a red sticker on the left side that reads, "I voted!" She pulls off her jacket, smiles, and says hi to me in the friendliest of manners, chewing a big white piece of gum all the while. She looks quite satisfied, having fulfilled her civic duty.

And this alone—this satisfaction of hers, this pleasure of chewing on her gum—this is enough to upset me. I feel a humiliating rage stirring deep within. I think I answer "Hi" in a very simple and unaffected way as I pass by her. But when she asks whether I am okay, I know I have allowed my frustration to take over me again. That is the second time in as many minutes. I turn to her and offer an apology. I'm sorry, I say, with a gesture of regret in my face and shaking my head, I'm just really busy.

I sit at my desk and spin my chair. I stuff my ears with loud music and submerge my head back into my cubicle—I am a sad, resentful ostrich fleeing from the bright and cheerful world beginning to blossom all around me.

Later, after all my coworkers have already left for lunch, I grab my sandwich. I need to get away from my desk. I retrieve my plastic bag and make my way to an office that is usually empty during lunchtime. Walking in, I am greeted by another coworker reading some preliminary exit polls on the computer. He turns to see me and says, quite unexpectedly, "I love you, N——!"

I reply, "¡Déjate de chingaderas!"

He wants to share his enthusiasm. I insult him in return. But it is all a calculated move. It is my best and only chance to spin myself in and out of that office, to avoid all conversation about the elections and to leave a cloud of mystery behind me all at once.

As I turn back, closing the door behind me with my right hand and my plastic bag in the other, I overhear him say jokingly, "¡Pinche N——!" His voice has a celebratory ring to it, and this annoys me even more.

I head out of the building and into the cool afternoon. I sit down on a bench, shivering under a generous November sun. Nibbling slowly at my sandwich, I hope for election day to soon be over.

I've never been so anxious to leave work. Usually, when the time to go home comes, I log off my computer, turn off my pager, turn off my cubicle light, pick up my backpack from the floor below my desk, and go. Though constantly under a latent threat, I trust Hesiod's maxim that "industry makes work go well, but a man who puts off work is always at hand-grips with ruin."

I am a fortunate man at ease. A man satisfied after completing another day's work.

I make my way up to the L. There, on the train platform, I am pleased and moved to see the crowds of enthusiastic people: young, old, black, white, hispanos, Asians all waiting for the train that will take them downtown.

Seeing that crowd, jovial and hopeful, I feel an overwhelming tenderness. I see their faces, their huge smiles—they are all so sure of themselves. For the past few months, they have been engaged in the making of history. Now, they are on their way to meet with it.

I see their faces and feel a tectonic movement rip some unknown, some unseen and unsuspected, latitude within me—I am glad to live in this city.

Thus am I immersed in my daydreaming when my train arrives. It goes in the opposite direction. It will take me back to my condo. I'll remain at the peripheries of history. I'll watch it unfold on my television screen.

I later find out that at least a couple of people I know have gotten tickets to go to Grant Park where Barack Obama is supposed to give a speech that night. I feel happy for them. One of them, Francisco, reaches me on the phone. He is excited almost to the point of agitation. He tells me about the two tickets he got and invites me along. That night the lights of the world would focus on one man. And there I'd be part of a jubilant and optimistic crowd. I, a mere shadow.

As I think of his invitation, I wonder whether the security personnel will have only metal detectors at the entrance. Will they card people at the gated area of Grant Park? Will they scan every ID? What would happen if I showed my fake driver's license? Would I be taken away quietly? Or would a police officer sound the alarm, imagining himself the hero that unraveled some wild conspiracy in which I am a key suspect? Who am I to ruin this wonderful night for Francisco?

I decline his invitation, and though my reasons for not going— like everything else about me—are false, I thank him sincerely. I tell him I have plans to meet some other people to celebrate, so I head downtown.

A quiet enthusiasm takes hold of me. Not knowing what else to do, I speed-dial my mother back in Guadalajara. I am ecstatic. Among other platitudes, I tell her that this is a night like no other. I tell her a new chapter of history is being written. As far as I am concerned, tonight Chicago is the center of the universe, and I am heading downtown to celebrate.

My mother tells me that Obama seems like a noble man and that he will make a good president. I concur with her and add that I am sure this time my situation will be solved once and for good.

Seasoned in the school of disappointment, she replies with wise skepticism, "Pues ojalá y sí, m'ijo."

The restaurant I walk into is packed, especially the bar area. I order a beer and am glad that I am not carded.

I sit down when a seat becomes available and watch on CNN how Pennsylvania has voted. And at that moment, we are all certain of what we knew all along—Barack Obama will be our next president.

And then people scream. Some clap and cheer. Some offer a toast. Someone weeps.

Two friends who are also downtown text me. They join me. We have a beer and then rush toward Grant Park.

In the distance, I see the word *USA* shining on the windows of an iconic building.

As if pulled by some gravitational force, I run toward the heart of the huge crowd. I run and run and stop at the metallic gates. In the distance, a huge television screen focuses the stage. Shortly after, Barack Obama comes out and says, "Hello, Chicago!"

Of the speech, I remember little or nothing, for I am seized by a very conflicting set of emotions. I stand there, overcome by an insurmountable sadness. I know that I, as a Mexican, will probably never see that kind of happiness or enthusiasm on the faces of my people, such optimism being contrary to our nature.

I hear the casual conversations of strangers converging on the lawn. Turning to see them, I know them to be the faces of transformation and unity, of faith in equality, and of a shared future. And for this moment, I feel deeply grateful.

All the obstacles I have run into during my life in this city, the unsought problems, the fifteen years of frustration I have been made to endure, all the lies I have hidden behind, all the fear, the humiliation, the stigma, the weight of this permanent yoke thrown upon my spirit—all of it begins to dissipate into the starry bosom of this cool November night.

The next day, at work, I will go back to the hiding, to my usual lying. Not the fleeing, the fanciful lie of election night, but the lie that sinks so deep in my mind that it hurts. I will resort, again, to cunning, that sinister and crooked wisdom Lord Francis Bacon writes about. On election night, however, surrounded by a cheerful sea of people, I feel propelled by the wings of victory. I feel my chest swell with pride and am just as American as anyone else around me.

SIX
THE DAY I GOT COUNTED

Some Other

"How about Samoan? Can I be Samoan?" My girlfriend is filling out the 2010 census. She is trying to answer the race question for me. The questionnaire came in the mail today. Ten years ago, when the previous census arrived, I glanced at it and tossed it in the garbage immediately. I was suspicious of it. This afternoon, however, I decided to leave it resting on the kitchen counter for a while.

As the evening went on, I couldn't help looking at the envelope from the corner of my right eye as I boiled the water, heated the oil, chopped the onions and peppers for dinner. It sat there, an innocuous piece of mail. I could have fed it to the paper shredder as soon as I got home, dismissed it like another piece of junk mail. And maybe I should have. But I couldn't muster the courage. Plus, my girlfriend would have eventually wondered why we never received it, as I'm sure she would want to fulfill her civic duty, to be included and counted.

I, having neither civic duty to fulfill nor moral obligation to live up to, had the luxury of ignoring it if I chose to do so. After all, what difference would it make if I didn't fill out the census? I, one single shadow unaccounted for amid millions more?

I glanced at the envelope again, first with resentment, then with amusement. What if I lied when answering it? However, in my midthirties now, I have bid good-bye to the irreverent youth who once disdained all things having to do with authority. The one who tore the previous census to pieces. A more mature man now, I want to come to terms with my situation.

The United States is well aware of my illegality. Yet it wants to count me in its numbers. Why? The United States has strict moral standards to live up to, and my inclusion in the census is an act of self-righteousness. An act perfectly consistent with the double morality of its discourse. The United States wants its house clean and orderly. A house where everyone is accounted for, even those living off the crumbs falling from its table.

While I still wasn't visible, when the clandestine nature of my status did not disturb it, the United States' social tension consisted mainly of an oscillating swing between racial opposites. Now it looks back on those days and wonders how on earth it grew so large, this middle shade I fall into. How should it solve this problem? My continued inclusion in the census is a stroke of genius in political correctness: it solves nothing, but it does give me the illusion of dignity while allowing the United States to pat itself on the back.

For more than a century now, the United States has been trying to sort out the Mexican question. Starting after the American invasion of Mexico, the definition of *Mexican* on the census forms has varied. Are Mexicans white or Indians? Another race altogether? Shall we relabel them as Latinos or Hispanic? It is as though, joining the effort of Mexico's brightest minds, the United States somehow has been dragged into the mess of trying to define Mexican identity.

Ten years ago, when I received the first census, I ducked and hid. The notion that the system that insisted on keeping me in the dark wanted me to acknowledge my presence *in writing* overnight was perplexing. That was then. Now I know better, and I have come to regard the census as one of those sweet ironies that make my life in this country more enjoyable. I imagine General Winfield Scott conquering Mexico, his triumphal entrance in the halls of Moctezuma.

Did he imagine this reversed and unarmed invasion I am a part of? Or what about Congress, during deliberations to annex "All Mexico," concluding that America could not absorb the whole of the Mexican population, some six or seven million at the time, because of our mongrel origin? What would they think of us Mexicans currently living in the country illegally, our numbers as high as the whole of our population back then? Or my favorite, the sententious statement of Ralph Waldo Emerson, ironically a fervent opponent of the American invasion of Mexico and a passionate admirer of ancient Mexico, that annexation of Mexico would "poison" Americans.

Mr. Emerson gave us Mexicans too much credit. Even if we ever plotted to poison the United States, our design would soon collapse. We Mexicans have consistently proven ourselves infallible at ruining our own grand goals. Our history is witness to our exceptional *in*capacity to carry any organized plan through its last consequences. So, to entertain Emerson's scenario of doomsday a little longer, a systematic plot to poison the United States would fail miserably. We could, at best, spice the crap out of its big belly and give it a bad case of diarrhea. But then, of course, our Catholic conscience would kick in, and we'd readily kneel to scrub its toilets.

"Well?" my girlfriend insists, pen in hand. Her clear blue eyes look attentively at me. The previous question was easy enough: "Yes, Mexican, Mexican Am., Chicano."

She goes on, reading my race options aloud. I can't really identify myself with any of them, so I pick Samoan. It seems remote, refreshing, exotic. An unconscious attempt to shake off my own exoticism. For what can be more exotic than a Mexican?

In college my Arab classmates often told me I looked like them. My two brothers look European. My grandmother has very distinctive indigenous features. I have a dark-complected aunt who has a daughter who looks completely Asian and a son who could pass as white.

Centuries of miscegenation have placed me out of the racial spectrum of the 2010 census. Thus, when I have to decide, I give up Samoan. I settle for the "Some other race" option. There is a second part to this question. I must *define* my race. I think about it for a minute, but the task bewilders my imagination. I throw my hands up in the air and tell my girlfriend to just leave the squares blank.

Fears and Dreams

Engaging with officialdom usually brings up some unpleasant affair. Every time I find myself treading into the dim abode of the sleeping beast, the experience is always the same—I am reminded of my situation, and a deep feeling of exclusion stirs within and unsettles me. The census underlines my origins, the place where I come from and to which I cannot return without putting a permanent seal on the life I have lived in the United States. It reminds me of my inability to travel, something I find particularly humiliating.

On other occasions, whenever I catch myself thinking about boarding a plane, it is not difficult to dissuade myself from such fantasies immediately. I think of the inconveniences of traveling: long lines, endless waiting, delays, lost luggage, jet lag; I try to convince myself that this subterranean turf I inhabit is better, that, over the terrifying immensity of the open skies, I prefer the concreteness of the ground, the safety, the guarantees it offers; I convince myself that I am more of the sedentary type and that to travel the world, I need not leave the hardened seat of this black wooden chair. However, deep down I know that, given a chance to fly, I'd be the first passenger checking his luggage. Boarding a plane would be a memorable event—a sense of deliverance those with traveling privileges and unaffected by the stigma of illegality can never understand. Something similar to what Emily Dickinson probably had in mind when she wrote about the sweetness of nectars, and the bitterness needed to truly enjoy them.

Thus, I have sought solace in this slow agony of writing. If nothing else, the ability to write is the one great gift all these years in the shadows have granted me.

The gift of dreaming. Writing to me has become a way of dreaming about things that seem near impossible. For instance, when President Obama visited my native Guadalajara in his first official trip to Mexico, I dreamed.

The three leaders of North America had, at last, reached an agreement that would allow us Mexicans the same traveling privileges that Americans and Canadians enjoy. Just like Canadians and Americans look forward to the charm of Mexican villages and the warmth and sun of our beaches, I too would look forward to strolling along the gloomy shores of Seattle, looking up at the imposing blue skies of Vancouver. I'd like to go skiing in Aspen; I'd like to lose myself in the melancholy explosion of a Vermont autumn. Feel the adrenaline rush of New York City.

But during that summit, no agreement to grant Mexican citizens traveling privileges was reached. *Los tres compadres* did, however, take some impressive pictures. In one of the pictures, the pointy leaves of a maguey stick out in the background. The three presidents sit quietly on beautiful handcrafted *equipales*. It is the first time Obama and Harper have drunk the maguey's honey, and now they seem happily absent. The security and growth of North America have been settled, and now they are just an American and a Canadian on vacation.

Greek Drama

Filling out official documents like the census can also be an act of hope. If only for a moment, I have stood at the threshold of legality and fancied that my life will be improved thenceforth. Spaces from which I have been excluded suddenly seem to open up their doors and offer a privileged place among people I have formerly looked at with envy. It is a momentary relief to years of uncertainty. But the mirage soon dispels—the inclusion of the undocumented in the census is simply a part of the grandiose moral gesture the United States wants for itself.

The disappointment that inevitably follows useless bureaucratic procedures does not, however, exhaust hope. Taking action is also a way of hoping. Actions like the rally of the spring of 2006 here in Chicago. Back then the future seemed promising for all of us leading a clandestine life. We were optimistic and didn't think it impossible to defeat the bigotry of the extreme Right. The Sensenbrenners, the Dobbses, and the Arpios wanted to portray us as base criminals. We wanted to show ourselves as hardworking people with the potential to have a real impact on society. That day seas of people chanted and cheered through the financial district of Chicago, swamping and paralyzing downtown. Reporters, perhaps exaggerating, wrote that the city had never witnessed anything similar.

It was an exciting experience, being in the crowd and seeing all those people marching in work clothes. Chef hats and factory uniforms were prevalent. But two years later, when our hopes were high and everything seemed on track for achieving comprehensive immigration reform, the Kennedy-McCain initiative dropped dead in the chambers of the House.

But the debate didn't stop there. Every politician knows that, come election year, the best way to gain free publicity is to take a position on the hot topic of immigration. I listen to their speeches. I know their opinions and arguments. For Democrats I am an undesired burden, for Republicans a replaceable nuisance. In the conservative discourse, I am a trespasser and a criminal—in their speeches, an abyss of moral rectitude separates me from the law-abiding citizen. Whenever the platform of a candidate has exhausted its creativity, whenever the polls show their numbers in decline, this is the kind of rhetoric we are likely to hear—a desperate appeal to moral rectitude.

Let them try to come out in my defense. Let them call me names. It is all a *show*. It comes down to *nothing*. They are all actors craving the spotlight, the microphones, the cameras!

This is a secret they won't tell but that I, in my shadowy fashion, have overheard—the *more* they speak of me and the *less* they do about me, the *more popular* they become. What geniuses! The louder they squabble, the brighter they shine! Wisely and with calculating cunning, they have reached a tacit agreement—that, when it comes to immigration, there will be no common agreement. Living on the surface has its benefits, its luxuries, and they are not willing to risk them. The world of pragmatic realpolitik, what does it care for this subterranean turf? Were legislators to vote their conscience, many would feel their smooth leather seats slip quickly away from under their comfortable assess.

It is so punctual, this biyearly cycle. It's got much of a Greek air to it, this festival of laughter and crying. And just how talented its actors are! How good at making *me* believe their play! The speed with which I build and watch the collapse of these castles in the air. But my daydreaming doesn't last long, and it is as ephemeral as hope.

Just this week, for instance, in a bipartisan effort similar to the Kennedy-McCain initiative, Senators Schumer and Graham published an editorial in favor of an immigration overhaul. Their initiative gained the immediate support of President Obama. Candidate Obama had promised an immigration bill within his first year in office. More than a year has gone by, and immigration reform has merited less of his time than the public deliberation about the ideal dog for the Obama family. One of the pillars of his domestic agenda during his campaign, immigration merited only one passing line in his first State of the Union address.

But I get it: the way has been hindered with obstacles. First, it was the economy. Then, the wars. Later unemployment; then health care. And now, the menacing shadow of midterm elections.

Yet there is hope. As I write these lines, an immigration rally is taking place in Washington, and those marching are optimistic. They believe in the strength of numbers, and they're putting up another show of power. It is no coincidence that this massive rally was scheduled for today, when the final vote on the health-care bill is expected.

The fate of any future immigration bill will depend on whether Republicans are willing to jeopardize the Hispanic vote again; whether the Tea Party will unleash a vicious campaign opposing and denouncing the legalization of more than twelve million "criminals"; whether, with unemployment at 10 percent, moderate Democrats will risk their cozy seats in Congress; whether a cowardly John McCain, pushed around and forced by the extreme Right to adopt an anti-immigrant stance, will return to his moderate self; whether the Hispanic caucus will vote yes on the health-care bill.

The mysterious ways of politics, how they make my head spin!

During the public debate about the future of immigration reform, a voice (a chatter box when it comes to every other subject in the galaxy) has been missing. New York, that beacon of light, has remained relatively silent. Whether the subject is just not interesting enough or it is too beneath her to be a topic of discussion at her cocktail parties and glossy editorial pages, only she knows. New York refuses to share her opinion. She remains aloof and unaffected. When I think of brainy New York and her empathy for the dilemma I find myself in, I am immediately reminded of one of her witty voices. In an interview with French Nobel laureate Jean-Marie Gustave Le Clézio, Adam Gopnik makes it clear just how distant the public intellectual has remained from the subject. Explaining how he ended up living in New Mexico, Le Clézio states that, after things got dangerous for his children in the Mexican state of Michoacán where he lived with his family, they, like most people in Mexico, just crossed the border into New Mexico. "*Not* in the back of a truck, though," Mr. Gopnik is quick to add, laughing, lest any of those present might get the wrong idea about Monsieur Le Clézio.

Had I been in the audience, how would *I* have felt? I have often caught myself asking this question. How would I have responded to Mr. Gopnik's derision, to all of his charged implications? I have thought about it often, but only now can I conclude that I probably would have felt nothing. My seventeen years of illegality have brought me face-to-face with every kind of humiliation, and this occasion need not be different—one more scar somewhere inside, invisible to the world because my skin has gotten so thick.

As I finish writing this thought, another question comes to mind—what on earth would *I* be doing at the PEN American Center anyway? Among cultured New Yorkers, I'd probably be nothing more than a mere curiosity, one that's infiltrated the learned chambers of the bourgeoisie, a wetback with intellectual pretensions.

But while immigration may be too pedestrian a thing to occupy herself with, New York sees eye to eye with Washington on the importance of other matters. Mr. Obama engages Americans in public deliberation over the best dog for the first family, and Mr. Gopnik meditates upon the nobility of dogs; while Mr. Obama flies his favorite chef—an expert, of all things, on Mexican food—into Washington from Chicago to have him prepare a state dinner, Mr. Gopnik indulges in and philosophizes about the virtues of French cuisine.

Mr. Obama's decadence reminds one of Moctezuma's sumptuous meals—more than three hundred dishes at a time—but it especially reminds one of Moctezuma's infallible foresight, of his fatalistic prophecy, the feeling that a life cycle was closing upon his floating, enchanted Tenochtitlán. Similarly, Earl Shorris reminds us that the shadow of evening is also here, creeping its way up the lawn of the Rose Garden. What disappeared from the world of the Aztec ruler was the element of magic, giving way to the sharp concreteness of steel and the wrath of four-legged gods. Now, however, what's been lost is the ethical component of politics. And, without ethics, Shorris tells us, politics has no limits.

Limitless power, President Obama has found, allows one to look, like Janus, in two different directions at once. And so every year Mr. Obama will likely throw a lavish Cinco de Mayo fiesta to commemorate "our shared heritage." He'll pick up his snifter and sip slowly on his aged tequila and then, with a single stroke of the same elegant left hand, sign a deportation slip worth four hundred thousand souls.

But let's forget about all that and allow Congress to debate the pending immigration bill. A bill whose fate will not depend on who has better arguments, but—like a wrestling match—on who can punch harder, scream louder. Like the fabled cat, the gluttons back in D.C. are not willing to go without food only because the cock can produce a lot of good reasons for not wanting to be eaten.

As the odds of Congress passing an immigration reform bill this year are slim, we'll surely live to see another fight. More bickering. A replay of this endless game. The continued spectacle of politics, this most civilized of butcheries.

Witnessing this recurring circus, I am reminded of a passage by Immanuel Kant where he writes that out of the crooked timber of humanity no straight thing was ever made. And, seized by the same feeling of impunity enjoyed by our politicians, I say to myself: *Fine—*

I'll be a greater cynic still! I'll fill out your papers, intensify my darkness, go deeper into the shadows!

After dinner, I look at my girlfriend again. She has picked up the census form and intends to finish filling it out. I ask her what she thought of dinner. She says it was okay and goes back to her scribbling. I am left thinking of the amount of spices and herbs I used in our dish—it had had a bittersweet tinge to it, and it was just a bit spicier than I would have liked it to be.

She is done with the census now, so I pick up the envelope and lick it. There is no dessert tonight, except this slimy thing, this sticky sensation on the tip of my tongue. I seal the envelope and feel quite satisfied—even if my situation goes unresolved for years, today, at least, I got counted.

POSTSCRIPT

When I got word that my book would be published, I knew I'd have to add to it. The previous chapters were written between 2008 and 2010. It is now September 2012. A final and more current chapter would give me an opportunity to write about crucial developments in my life having to do with my new family and my employment during these past two years. This postscript would also help me come to terms, once and for all, with the peculiar situation I have found myself in since my arrival in Chicago almost two decades ago.

The first event of great importance in my life during this period was my marriage. My wife, D——, and I got married on an autumn day, which in Chicago usually means chilly weather and cloudy gray skies. That day, though, everything that was gloomy and cold about Chicago disappeared. The skies opened up, and instead of the taciturn spectacle of autumn, we were graced with the warmth of a perfectly mild summer day. Among the many pictures the photographer took, there is one where we are standing by the iconic "bean" at Millennium Park. In the picture, you can see the pride of the city, the reflection of the Chicago skyline, that cluster of glass and steel that rises vertically with impunity and indifference to all things human. We are looking in the direction of the skyline, but we are really looking past it and into a blue and cloudless horizon. I took the clear skies in the picture as the first sign of a promising future. We looked forward to our married life with expectation and optimism.

Just minutes earlier, D—— arrived at a previously chosen place where the picture session would start. We had been here on numerous occasions before, strolling along the colonnades, sitting among the exuberant vegetation and huge flower pots—taller than us—admiring the well-tended gardens stretching south, and finally sinking into and blending with a curving Lake Shore Drive, at the end of which you can see the Museum Campus.

There is a very Roman air to this part of town. I was sitting on a bench, looking at the classical architecture around me, when I saw her. She was walking toward me. Her hair was pulled back in a French chignon. She was wearing a dress the color of pearls, her upper chest was exposed and it looked smooth and delicate, her hands were wrapped tightly around a bright bouquet, and she smiled graciously. That was what I first saw from a distance. I walked up to meet her. I could better see her face then, and it was radiant and youthful. Her smile was wide and perfect—two subtle dimples added a touch of sophisticated innocence to her face. I looked into her eyes, those eyes of an impossible blue whose depth and clarity I've come to regard as my one and only solace in the uncertain world I inhabit, and I wanted to say something, but I remained silent. Some things are better left unspoken.

Briefly after, we were at the Chicago Cultural Center getting married. Outside, the red autumn foliage burned against the shiny steel of the music pavilion at Millennium Park. Inside, the ceremony took place. The woman about to be my wife stood in front of me, repeating the solemn matrimonial vows after the judge. And as I heard her voice, I felt grateful to the point of nervousness. D—— noticed and smiled with the same calm and intent she's used to reassure me throughout our relationship, since that evening when, embarrassed and vulnerable, I revealed my unauthorized migratory status to her. I felt her hand, soft and compassionate, reaching for mine. She was aware of just how difficult things might get for us going forward. Yet she smiled with confidence as she slid the ring on my finger. What a great and humbling gift this is, to be welcomed in someone else's life, to be accepted unconditionally. And just how lucky one is to find the one person in the world willing to share one's burden, the person who will get to see you at your best and worst, the one who will know your weaknesses and arrogance like no one else, the one who completes you in more than one sense.

Despite having planned our wedding in a matter of weeks rather than months, everything turned out just as we imagined. Ours was a small and modest reception, but the most sumptuous of feasts couldn't have made me happier. We chose the back room of our favorite restaurant, a place barely big enough to accommodate a small number of guests. D——'s family, her relatives, and friends came from out of town. I invited a few friends, some coworkers, and my closest relatives. Never had the absence of my mother, my brothers, and my immediate family been more difficult. Yet I glowed with happiness.

As we sat at the table, I thought of my mother, the phone call I had received from her that morning. I thought of the many, many years that had passed since we had seen each other in person. I thought of my father. I tried to imagine their own wedding, their short marriage, doomed from early on by the looming shadow of my father's untimely death.

The sad and prolonged echo of a trumpet brought me back. This was the music my parents liked listening to, a song my father used to court my mother with. Our decision to hire a trio to play at our wedding was a way of paying homage to my absent parents. The songs I asked the musicians to play were all boleros I learned from my mother's own singing. D—— had suggested that we try to get my mother a visa to come to our wedding. But I had already built up my mother's expectations like this before, only to have her hopes crushed at the American consulate. Heck, even my aging grandmother had met the indifference, the suspicion and rejection, of the American officials in Guadalajara who were just as eager to take her application money as they were to send her out in disappointment. Perhaps this time would be different if I write a letter and promise to be fully responsible for your mother's expenses and return, D—— had said.

But there was really nothing she could do—her two-hundred-plus years of family history in this country would not count for anything when trying to fix the situation of her future husband, let alone that of his Mexican family.

But my mother had already made her peace, and she would be happy to watch her son's wedding on video.

As I write these pages, we have been married almost two years. For some reason, since we first started dating, everything in our lives started happening at a rhythm we didn't expect. Like a Vivaldi concerto, a new layer of our lives began unfolding with each season. In summer we got engaged. By fall we were married. In winter we were expecting our baby. It was almost as though we were trying to make up for all the time we didn't know each other.

Then came spring, replete with promises.

We both had stable jobs, we were still living in my condo, and my wife had just taken a mortgage on a house. It was an old house in need of major renovation. It was there that the projects of spring would blossom. It would be months before we could move in, but the sheer idea filled us with excitement. It was the house we wanted. We chose it carefully, considering its potential. We were going to have a porch and a backyard ready for the arrival of our baby. Also important to us was its location—it was close to my wife's work and only a couple of blocks from the train so I could take it to work every day.

One pleasantly cool April evening, D—— was trying on some new maternity clothes. I was sitting at the end of our bed, swinging my legs like at the edge of a cliff, watching—her pregnancy had accentuated her beauty; she *was* happiness itself, her face radiating with life. She continued to try her clothes on, and the childish sparkle in her eyes told me this was not a good time to interrupt. I needed to tell her about an important change in our lives taking place that month.

April, we all know, is the cruelest month.

:::

The new head of human resources at work decided upon arriving that some order was needed in his new house. Within only a few weeks of getting the job, he cut loose the fine thread that had been holding Damocles' sword as a latent threat above my head. And, as all things Greek, the blade was destined to fulfill its fate. One Thursday evening, it finally fell, and my head came rolling down the office where I'd been working and hiding for the past five years. The e-mail I received demanded that I clarify a problem with my Social Security number. It gave me only a few days.

I had been dreading this day since I first got the job. I had imagined different scenarios, which varied from the truly civilized to the highly embarrassing, from an uncomfortable meeting in my manager's office to the abrupt arrival of the security guard behind my chair, ordering me to pack up my things and follow him outside immediately without offering any explanation as to why. But everything happened so quickly and was so impersonal that the only thing I could think of doing was to respond the same way. So, toward the end of the day, I prepared my letter of resignation, effective immediately. The following day, I turned it in and never went back to work again.

By the time this book comes out, it will be more than two years since I lost my job. And during this time, I have often wondered how they see me, my superiors, what they think of me. In my resignation letter, I thanked them for their support and explained that I was leaving to start my own company. I suppose for them my departure was as abrupt as it was puzzling. What kind of nonsense got hold of this guy? they probably wondered at the time. I had never missed one day of work during my five years of employment. So a decision like this, leaving a stable and well-paying job, where both colleagues and superiors had showed me nothing but respect, was way out of character for me, especially considering that my wife was pregnant at the time, that she had just taken a mortgage on our new house, and that I myself had my condo mortgage to pay. I was gambling my family's future to embark on an uncertain business venture.

The next day, on Friday, I waited deliberately until everyone left the office to avoid saying good-bye to my coworkers or having to offer any explanations about my rushed decision. I wanted to avoid sad faces and curious inquiries into or genuine concerns about my personal life. We had shared some good laughs at that office, and that was what I wanted to take with me. And my bosses? They had been exceptionally welcoming and supportive, always treating me fairly. Six months earlier, they had seen me elated, at my wedding. And now I couldn't get myself to look them straight in the face. Better to let them think of me as an ungrateful bastard than to reveal to them the reality that stigmatizes me, better to disappoint them by leaving my job suddenly and without apologies than to implicate them in this mess I find myself in, better to let them have an unfavorable opinion of me than to have them feel pity and helplessness in the face of my situation. My superiors—the earthly trinity whose names I must omit here, but to whom I am greatly indebted both because of their professional support and their invaluable friendship.

Thus, assaulted by feelings of guilt and failure, that Friday evening I took down the wedding pictures I had pinned on my cubicle and gathered my personal belongings. I printed the letter of resignation I had prepared the night before and went to my manager's mailbox. There, I dropped it off along with my pager and my badge and my keys and everything that had made me a part of that organization, everything that I thought was mine. I looked around to see if anyone was still there, but everyone was gone for the weekend. I turned off the lights and looked back one last time—everything was quiet and dark in the office. I had entered that company with the stealth of a thief, and like a thief I left.

::::

Losing my job like that was devastating. I felt humiliated. The idea of not being able to provide for my family depressed me: it was an emasculating feeling I had never experienced before. And, with immigration laws becoming more and more stringent all the time and companies implementing sophisticated electronic methods to check the employability of potential candidates, my hopes of ever being hired as a professional translator again became dimmer and dimmer. The only hope for me was to regularize my situation, but under the current laws it is simply impossible. Never mind that I studied English and put myself through college and grad school, strict prerequisites every politician attempting to fix the immigration problem always places on top of his demands for migrants. Never mind that, after paying my taxes punctually for almost two decades, at the end of every year I get a letter from the Social Security Administration stating that the amount they have retained for that particular year will not be credited to my retirement fund (the most recent letter telling me the total amount accumulated during all these years just came recently in the mail, but I no longer bothered to open it). Never mind all that. Let us focus on the present, on the one thing that would solve my problem once and for all—a sound and sensible reform of the current immigration system, pretty much like what candidate Obama promised during his presidential campaign.

But now, almost at the end of his term, we shouldn't deceive ourselves anymore: President Obama does not much care about the plight of undocumented immigrants. Quite the contrary—his administration has been particularly vicious when it comes to this issue. Since President Obama took office, the rate of deportation has risen exponentially, surpassing by a great margin that of his Republican predecessor. How far were we from imagining we'd be dealing with the aftermath of broken families—fathers handcuffed and dragged out of their houses in the middle of the night, babies snatched from the arms of their weeping mothers—when candidate Obama courted the Latino vote with the promise to reform the immigration system within his first year in office! Not only has the deportation rate increased during his term. Mr. Obama never intended to make good on his promise—one, two, three, and now almost four years have passed since he took office. He didn't have the will to do it with a Democratic Congress, and he won't do it now. Some liberal president this is!

And now, even with his hands bound tight by a Republican Congress, there is still much Mr. Obama could do, as shown by his recent move to regularize the situation of the so-called Dreamers. But those who see in this action a brave political move or an act of empathy on the part of Mr. Obama deceive themselves. We should see and judge things for what they are. To even entertain the idea that Mr. Obama had an epiphany about the use of his executive powers is to be blind and naive. Let us remember the favorite two-second sound bite politicians from both parties use indiscriminately when talking about immigration, "This is a nation of laws, but we are also a compassionate people." Such a clever line, an aura of rectitude and empathy that makes us recover our faith in the benevolence of politics. But politics has no heart. It is a cold and calculated game. And just so, there is nothing generous or humane in Mr. Obama's latest action. Otherwise, why prolong the agony of the "children" in question for more than three years?

It is clear that executive power alone is not enough to reform the immigration system. What is not clear is Mr. Obama's unwillingness to better use it to alleviate the lives of millions more people. No, it is not clear, but I believe we all have a pretty good idea—with his move to help the "Dreamers," it is President Obama's conviction that he has done enough to appease the outrage of Latino voters, thus pocketing a key constituency in swing states in the coming presidential election.

In an election year, an immigration overhaul is too volatile a topic to take on, just like it was during his first year in office. This is probably the wise counsel President Obama received from Rahm Emanuel, who worked tirelessly on anti-immigrant measures before becoming Obama's chief of staff.

Larger interests always lurk behind every political move. That's why I wasn't surprised to read recently that Mr. Emanuel, now the respectable mayor of this great city of Chicago, has created a new office at city hall, the "Office of New Americans." Mr. Emanuel wants to make of Chicago the "most immigrant-friendly city" in the world! But in his initiatives, nothing in favor of undocumented immigrants is mentioned. A small step, like offering official IDs to the undocumented, would go a long way for those who could benefit. But he wants nothing to do with that. His goal is to unleash the entrepreneurial potential of "new" Americans, that is, of those who already have their papers in order. But then we have to remember that Mayor Emanuel is no friend of the undocumented. As a leading member of the Democratic Party, he urged Democrats in close races to support the Sensenbrenner bill that demonized people like me, made me a criminal, pushed me deeper in the shadows.

And now—is Mr. Emanuel's sight already set on higher office?—he has decided to confront President Obama's position on the detention of undocumented immigrants, an initiative for which Emanuel himself advocated.

: : :

My wife and I moved into our new house at the beginning of the summer of 2011, and, though the contractor had finished a lot of renovations, there was still much to do. I might not have had a job anymore, but what I did have was free time. D—— was on vacation, and our days were consumed by running errands and finding new furniture. At that rate, I soon realized, my savings of the past five years wouldn't last long. But spending them in this house was an investment I hoped would pay off in the future. Meanwhile, we kept shuffling through endless cards of new paint colors. We had decided to repaint our baby's room in bright but neutral tones because we didn't know its gender and had no plans to find out.

Another project that occupied my time was our backyard. Hitherto, I'd never had any interest in any sort of vegetation, but even a person like me knew that the aggressive weeds that had taken over the lawn in our backyard needed to go. There was a huge pine tree in need of trimming, plants to choose, a whole vegetable garden to cultivate. Cicero once wrote that all a man ever needs in order to be happy is a garden and a library. For some years, I'd owned a modest library. When I wanted to withdraw from the world, I'd flee there and dedicate countless hours to witnessing the adventure of life springing, sometimes wildly and other times quietly, from within. But those days last summer, what mesmerized me most was the sight of green, nourishing life as it arose from what used to be nothing more than a fractured concrete bed, the former parking spot of a small car or a motorcycle.

One afternoon, rinsing the tomatoes and bell peppers and jalapeños I'd just picked from our garden, I turned to the living room. D—— was sitting on the couch, looking down at her growing belly, rubbing it slowly, her tired legs stretched out on top of the coffee table. I thought of the Roman sage again and said to myself that, in his estimation of a man's happiness, an essential component, one's family, is missing.

We had been living in our new house for only a couple of months when D——'s doctor ordered her onto full bed rest. It was during the following months that I discovered the true joy and humility of a domestic life. I learned, for instance, that there are times when a man's personal ambition and frustrated goals become truly insignificant, that there are crucial moments when, before the larger designs of life, one must bend one's neck and be a mere instrument, and that to oppose any of the changes time brings about amounts to ingratitude and blasphemy toward life.

During those summer months, we sat together for hours and hours. We'd have dinner on our porch and look at the yellow and purple and orange flowers in the backyard and the vegetables ripening; we'd smell the basil growing disproportionately some twenty feet away from us and listen to the leaves of the crabapple tree serenading us whenever a gentle breeze cruised by.

Later at night, in the living room, I would sit at D——'s feet. She would eat ice cream while we listened to quiet music. Rubbing her feet gently, I would joke about my indentured servitude, how I hoped it would pay for my passage into the bright side of American society at some point in the future. We'd laugh and then go on to deliberate the long lists of names she was considering for our baby. My own list was rather short—if it was a boy, I wanted the name of a German composer, a Danish philosopher, or a Mexican poet. If it was a girl, her middle name would be of Nahuatl origin. Our baby's room was ready by then, and the colors were brighter, the walls covered with stickers of the alphabet and trees and animals: a three-dimensional bird fluttered its turquoise feathery wings on top of the changing table.

A few weeks later, when our baby had decided it was time to come, I looked at my wife right after the delivery. She was exhausted and beaten. But when she was handed our baby and held her for the first time, her face transformed, and there was no trace of tiredness or pain, only an immense smile full of gratitude, a smile humbled by the mystery of life she'd had the privilege to perpetuate.

The next day, at the special care nursery, I held my little daughter in my arms. She was so small and vulnerable. Her head was full of black hair. She had the perfectly and delicately arched eyebrows of her mother and, when she yawned, at the bottom of those chubby cheeks I could tell she would inherit her elegant dimples as well. I was thus admiring this new little person sleeping quietly in my arms when the miracle happened: I saw her big, dark, and curious eyes open for the first time and look attentively at me, like asking: Who are you? What are you doing here?

::::

Anybody who has read this far into my book will agree that my personal situation is rather unusual for a Mexican immigrant. I will be the first one to acknowledge the peculiarity of my circumstances. I have been lucky enough to find my way into the social fabric of the United States, and this is my satisfaction and my loss. The world I knew when I first came to the United States has been turned on its head. The person I was has been completely transformed. Now, when I contemplate the adventure of the young immigrant breaking through the border almost two decades ago, he is almost unrecognizable. Such boldness, such confidence in the face of uncertainty. I think of him now and can't help but feel nostalgic—he is as ambitious as he is naive, his head full with pecuniary ideas. In more than one sense, he fits the profile of the typical Mexican immigrant perfectly—his education is minimal, and he comes from a socially disadvantaged family; like most migrants, he is driven by earthly ambition and believes the mere access to the United States, even if it means sneaking through its back door, to be the panacea for all his problems. He has no idea what the future has in store for him: going from one menial job to another, learning English, going to college, becoming a professional translator, owning a condo, writing a book, getting married, losing his job, and becoming a father are all things he can't imagine at the time of his transgression.

All he can think of is the endless night before him, the heavy legs, the promises that await him on the other side. So he runs and runs until he disappears into the darkness, into the long night of America.

Every aspect of my life I have written about in this book has permanently altered me. Throughout the years, the naïveté of the young immigrant who crossed the border has been gradually disappearing.

Experience has taught me that presence in the land of plenty and a relatively stable job aren't enough to make one happy. And hence, other more traditional traits of both my new home and my country of origin have been slowly reshaping the person I've become.

I am the product of an unlikely encounter—American optimism and Mexican cunning brawl within me. Like the roots of two different plants, these opposing characteristics have become accomplices in a subterranean struggle, one nourishing the life that stretches jovially toward the surface and the light, the other reaching ever deeper downward, as if to negate the first. The mixed result is that I don't feel quite at home with either way of being. Yet I need both. I *am* both. With one foot in the light and the other in the shadows, I tiptoe between both worlds, squinting and averting my eyes when the brightness becomes too intense and artificial, or feeling overwhelmed when the darkness gets too depressing and threatening. And it is only moving at this tempo, at the rhythm of this two-step dance of estrangement, that I feel at ease. Pretty much like the commelinas snuggling against the shady fence in my backyard, eager to open up their purple petals to the intermediate light, but just as quick to close up tightly when the full sunlight descends upon them.

: : :

The main lesson my American experience has taught me is that of possibility. It was in the writings of Ralph Waldo Emerson that I got my first glimpse of the American character, so blatantly different from my own, so daring, so confident in the power to take charge of one's own life and destiny.

For many years, the counsel I found in his pages was the guiding principle that helped me get this far. But after the momentous developments in my life in the past two years, the demands on me are now different. I am totally involved, first, in the care of my daughter; then, in that of my house; and later, in the overall improvement of the neighborhood.

In the evenings, after I have been home with my daughter tending to her needs all day and trying to figure out a way to find employment to no avail, D—— gets back from her job, and I head out to the backyard. The work in that little universe is never ending. One evening, after spending an hour or two there, weeding the flower beds, pruning the rose bushes and the crabapple tree, watering the grass, picking the new vegetables, I come back in the house. The house we may not even get to keep, our income having been sliced in half after I lost my job. Nighttime is approaching, and my whole day has been consumed in domestic chores. Realizing how late it is, I complain and complain to D—— that I no longer have time to do anything anymore. I'd like to go running, take long walks. But what hurts the most is thinking of my books in the basement going unread, getting dusty. And I know that by doing this, I am being ungrateful. But I am also a frustrated man, unable as I am to get a job that pays enough to support this family and this new house. D—— looks tired. She's had a long and stressful day at work. Her eyes are heavy from lack of sleep. Looking at her and my little daughter falling asleep in her arms, I feel utterly ashamed of myself. Not once has she complained about her own burden, the responsibilities she's assumed as head of the family. What she has lamented and very deeply is having to leave her daughter when the time came for her to go back to work after maternity leave. This family is upside down, and for this I feel guilty and responsible and helpless, and, at the same time, I feel grateful for my wife and daughter, and all I can do when I find the time is sit here and type. But how can I repay in writing the kindness I've received in life?

:::

Emerson, the sage of Concord, might have put lofty ideas in my head, but it was only thanks to the Mexican cunning in my DNA that I was able to infiltrate spaces that otherwise would have been inaccessible to me. We Mexicans are masters of backdoor deals. Even to date, when the advantages of the digital age are supposed to make the transparency of any process of public concern an easy task, our most public of processes, the Mexican presidential election, is still decided behind closed doors. In a country where 98 percent of reported crimes go unpunished, this should come as no surprise. We Mexicans enjoy a long tradition of impunity that fosters corruption at all levels of society. During my twenty years of life in Mexico, I never met one single person willing to let the transit police officer take away his driver's license when he could avoid the nuisance involved by bribing the officer. Nor have I ever heard of any officer refusing the bribe, regardless of how little it might be.

It is out of the collision of these two opposing ideas—the belief in possibility, the recourse of the lie—that the new person that I am has come into being. Which is not to say that my passage between the one world and the other is now effortless. Many a time, confused either by cultural idiosyncrasies or by a complex dialogue, I turn my perplexed face to my secret sharer and ask for clarification, "A ver güerita, explícame qué quiso decir ella con eso."

My experience has also taught me that the alleged fairness of American institutions is, like the benevolence of its founding fathers, rather mythical. But that which officialdom has denied me, I have found in the hearth of my own home. In the eyes of my wife, I have met the legendary generosity of the United States that otherwise I have found only in political speeches and indoctrinating textbooks.

It is thanks to my wife that I have become more involved in the civic life of the city, participating in neighborhood meetings, in efforts to clean the streets, keep them safe. Just the other day I received a phone call from our alderman's office. They were getting back to me about an inquiry I had made regarding an abandoned KFC building that's become the hangout for bums. I am worried about its appearance, how it could affect the area. I wanted to find out if they were doing anything to bring a new business to open there. One of the things that bothered my wife when we first moved to this house was that the block had very few trees. So this fall, after persistently bugging the city, I finally got them to plant new trees on the whole block.

Sometimes American optimism takes such a hold of me, it is annoying even to my wife. Taking a stroll with our daughter in the better part of the neighborhood, by the river, where traders and executives and surgeons live, I see a chance to show off my new knowledge and go into a craze naming some of the trees there, both the native and the exotic (D——— rolls her eyes in anticipation). I like the mysterious bark of the sycamore, how it peels like a snake, how fat its trunk gets, the pale green of its leaves, how massive the whole thing grows. On the opposite end, about a certain variety of the Japanese maple, it is truly amazing to see its inversion of colors, how it goes from being burgundy in the spring to green in the fall; also interesting is how tiny and compact it is, how, how, how . . . I can't find the word I'm looking for, so I ask D—— for help. "Frondoso," I tell her, stretching out my arms and curving my hands, like holding a huge beach ball. How do you say that? "Leafy," she answers. "*Leafy?*" I scoff, unconvinced. English always has *so many* words for everything. There surely ought to be another one that resembles the Spanish more. The repeating "O's" of the Spanish word, I say, give it a sound that is both aggressive and terrifying, a sound that evokes images of jungles and caves and echoes of manly primitive chants. I then get down on my knees in front of the stroller and repeat to my daughter, in long and exaggerated syllables: FROOON-DOO-SO, FROOON-DOO-SO. But she is too busy looking at two squirrels chasing each other in the huge lawn of the house to our right. Then, looking up toward the treetops gracing our walk with a cool shade, I tell D—— that one day our block will look just like this. She smiles with skepticism. Next time I talk to my mother on Skype, I am outraged at a news report I have recently read. I give her an earful about "those people" who mutilated the purple crowns of thirty blooming *jacarandas* in the Guadalajara highway going to the airport just so the billboards could be read from the road below. "¡Pinches animales!" I say to her.

This summer, in the early evenings, I go out to water the grass and our small garden in front of the house. I see our neighbors, the old residents of this block. This neighborhood, my wife tells me, is one of the most diverse in the city. There are people from Puerto Rico, the Philippines, Eastern Europe, South America, the Middle East, Africa. Early in the spring, they first saw me reseeding the grass. Then, watering our new trees. Then they saw me telling the landscapers I wanted the antiquated Japanese yews removed. Now they see me come out and water the blooming plants and the new grass. What do they think of me? So far, they probably think I just like spending time outdoors in the summer. But in a few years, when the impending gentrification takes place, these old residents—most of whom are retired and most likely live on their Social Security checks—will probably blame me for that.

It is 6:10 in the evening, and another type of people begins to walk by. They are the new residents on this block, young professionals coming back from work in the Loop (why *aren't* they involved in the neighborhood committee?). Sometimes, when I take my daughter out for a morning stroll in the neighborhood, I see them leave.

Not long ago, you couldn't tell me apart from them, riding on the L to work. But now I spend most of my time at home, and by the time they come back, I am almost done watering the grass. They say hi and I smile back. I look happy and proud when they comment on how great our colorful little garden is looking, but when they go past me I feel envious. It is the same old envy of the busboy looking at those dining at the next table as he leans over to pick up plates, wipe off crumbs, rearrange chairs.

Then I look up at the window. My wife and daughter are standing there. My daughter, whose name means Clear Star, has just learned to wave hi, and she is waving enthusiastically at me now. I wave back.

We reflect the diversity of this neighborhood perfectly. We are a bilingual family. We are a modern family: a white American woman who goes off to work in the mornings and a minority man with an accent staying home to care for their baby. Anybody observing us would immediately think just how lucky we are, what a perfect life we live. But of the uncertainty that reigns inside this house, of this helplessness that swells like a balloon, of the darkness that looms large at every moment—that they know nothing about. And it is better that way. Better to have them think of us as extraordinary than for them to look at us with pity and commiseration.

I catch myself rehearsing this inner monologue when I notice that many of the leaves on the small smoketree I recently planted are not doing so well—they look brown and sad and dry, and my hope is that that little tree will make it through this year. I come up to it with the intention to prune it. I kneel to make a clean cut, and then I see two small leaves of a bright lime green shooting out at the bottom of a decaying branch—such a little tree and such a complicated life! I look up and see my wife and daughter again. They're smiling now. I cut off the dying part of the branch and leave the new leaves exposed. Tomorrow morning they'll get direct southern exposure. I place the pruners in my back pocket. My work out in the garden is done for the day.

Before going back into the house, I look up the window and feel comforted by the sight of my wife and daughter—like two heavenly sentinels looking over this limbo I inhabit, they have been hovering by the window, watching me the whole time.

JOSÉ ÁNGEL N. is an undocumented immigrant. He lives in Chicago.

LATINOS IN CHICAGO AND THE MIDWEST

Pots of Promise: Mexicans and Pottery
at Hull-House, 1920–40 *Edited by Cheryl R. Ganz and Margaret Strobel*
Moving Beyond Borders: Julian Samora and the Establishment
of Latino Studies *Edited by Alberto López Pulido,
Barbara Driscoll de Alvarado, and Carmen Samora*
¡Marcha! Latino Chicago and the Immigrant Rights Movement
Edited by Amalia Pallares and Nilda Flores-González
Bringing Aztlán to Chicago: My Life, My Work, My Art
*José Gamaliel González, edited and with an Introduction
by Marc Zimmerman*
Latino Urban Ethnography and the Work
of Elena Padilla *Edited by Mérida M. Rúa*
Defending Their Own in the Cold: The Cultural Turns
of U.S. Puerto Ricans *Marc Zimmerman*
Chicanas of 18th Street: Narratives of a Movement
from Latino Chicago *Leonard G. Ramírez with Yenelli Flores,
María Gamboa, Isaura González, Victoria Pérez,
Magda Ramírez-Castañeda, and Cristina Vital*
Compañeros: Latino Activists in the Face of AIDS *Jesus Ramirez-Valles*
Illegal: Reflections of an Undocumented Immigrant *José Ángel N.*

The University of Illinois Press
is a founding member of the
Association of American University Presses.

Composed in 10/14 Sabon LT Std
with Helvetica Neue display
by Lisa Connery
at the University of Illinois Press
Manufactured by Thomson-Shore, Inc.

University of Illinois Press
1325 South Oak Street
Champaign, IL 61820-6903
www.press.uillinois.edu